PUDDIN'

PUDDIN'

LUSCIOUS AND UNFORGETTABLE PUDDINGS,

PARFAITS, PUDDING CAKES, PIES, AND POPS

. . .

CLIO GOODMAN

with ADEENA SUSSMAN

SPIEGEL & GRAU

NEW YORK

Published in the United States by Spiegel & Grau,
an imprint of The Random House Publishing Group,
a division of Random House, Inc., New York.

SPIEGEL & GRAU and the HOUSE colophon are registered trademarks
of Random House, Inc.

Photos on pages xx, 20, 45, 46, 72, and 128
are by Larissa Drekonja and are used by permission.

LIBRARY OF CONGRESS CATALOGING-IN-PUBLICATION DATA

Goodman, Clio.
Puddin' : luscious and unforgettable puddings,
parfaits, pudding cakes, pies, and pops /
Clio Goodman ; with Adeena Sussman.
pages   cm
ISBN 978-0-8129-9419-3 —ISBN 978-0-8129-9420-9 (ebook)
1. Puddings. 2. Desserts. I. Sussman, Adeena. II. Title.
TX773.G648 2013
641.86'44—dc23   2013004255

Printed in China on acid-free paper

www.spiegelandgrau.com

2 4 6 8 9 7 5 3 1

FIRST EDITION

Book design by Barbara M. Bachman

For my family and friends,
for encouraging and believing in
all of my crazy ideas

CONTENTS

CHAPTER 3: TOPPINGS

COOKIES AND CAKE TOPPINGS

SAUCES, COMPOTES, AND TOPPINGS

INTRODUCTION

. . . .

I NEVER EXPECTED TO OPEN A DESSERT SHOP DEVOTED TO PUDDING, but I guess if you look closely, the signs were always there. Most children get caught with their hand in the cookie jar. Me? I was the kid filling *up* the cookie jar with the sneak-worthy treats.

I grew up in a family of food-loving artists and musicians, with my grandfather's masterly paintings staging the backdrop for meals prepared by my mother. Music was supplied by my dad, who can play just about any instrument handed to him, as my brother, Emmett, and I sketched cartoons furiously in the corner. When it comes to food, my mom, Hevra, has always been a kitchen-based Harriet the Spy. She doesn't just cook; she makes a point to learn about every recipe she's mastering, researching and taking meticulous, almost scholarly notes. Every new dish is accompanied by curated information repeated devotionally at the table. In addition to encouraging my love of drawing and cartoons, Mom detected an early interest in baking. She bought me dessert kits, books, magazines, exciting ingredients—art supplies for the budding pastry wonk.

Weekends and after-school hours were spent scouring the Internet and reading cookbooks, immersing myself in marathon baking sessions that left me covered in powdered sugar, and rolling fondant, scribbling notes, and illustrating my adventures. The best part was feeding my family the sweets of my labor. They were a willing but honest audience. The compliments came alongside constructive criticism that helped me grow and prepared me for a life in desserts.

This sugar-dusted upbringing led me to the Culinary Institute of America, where I studied baking and pastry arts and discovered that much of the curriculum consisted of things Mom had already schooled me on at home. With my upbringing as my ballast, I felt free to sail creatively. I viewed the entire pastry-school experience as one massive art project with scientific and culinary underpinnings. "I don't know what I want to make, but this is what I want it to look like," I'd tell my professors, who would shake their heads, then move away as I dreamed in sugar, flour, and vanilla.

After school I ended up working as a pastry chef at New York's famous Union Square Café, which laid the groundwork for my future. There I learned to balance an artist's short attention span with a restaurant worker's discipline, teamwork, and long hours.

Once I left Union Square I began working as a private chef for the brother of a friend of mine. I cooked everything for him, from daily meals to elaborate dinner parties attended by dozens. One night I served pudding for dessert. I'd made it growing up, loving the way a few simple ingredients—milk, sugar, eggs, and cornstarch—could come together to create something so simultaneously elegant and comforting. My chocolate pudding became his house dessert, stocked at all times in his fridge and much in demand by his friends and colleagues.

Eventually I went into business with him, opening a tiny shop in New York's East Village that sells pudding—but distributes good cheer to the neighborhood free of charge. The days before the shop opened were sheer madness, with me developing recipes around the clock, and a manic schedule and shoestring budget conspiring against us. But we opened on time and sold out of all our wares that very first day in January 2012.

Everything we sell at Puddin'—and I mean *everything*—is house-made, from (of course) the puddings, cakes, and cookies to the confetti-like sprinkles to the graham crackers, fudge sauce, and marshmallow crème. They would be easier to buy, but that's just not my way. I view every recipe as a labor of love, worked on and tweaked until it meets my standards, specifications, and creative vision. All of those recipes, and many more, are here in these pages. There are classic puddings you'd expect, such as chocolate, vanilla, and banana, and more unexpected flavors, including cashew, passion fruit, and malted milk. Then there are cakes, parfaits, sauces, and condiments that are the edible expression of my culinary dreams. I know I may be biased, but they're all pretty irresistible. I hope you love them as much as I do. Happy puddin'!

PUDDING 101

THE GREAT THING ABOUT MOST OF THESE RECIPES IS JUST HOW SIMPLE they are. If you're anything like me, you'll marvel every time at the magic that occurs when a few steps come together to create something so fantastic. You may already have many of the ingredients in your home, and most of what I call for is easy to find. But there are some basic principles you should follow when making pudding. Think of these guidelines as friendly tips from someone who learned the hard way, through trial and error and hundreds of iterations. If you didn't read any of them, you'd figure it out for yourself, but I want you to have success with your very first batch!

Pudding 101

Choose Quality.

Great ingredients yield stellar results. It's the cardinal rule of cooking, so try to use the best-quality milk, eggs, and fruit you can find. That being said, these recipes work with staples you probably already have in the house, making them supremely convenient to produce.

Mix It Up.

Always, always, *always* mix your milk and other ingredients while they are very cold, and make sure you're working away from any heat source. In order for the cornstarch to really do the important job of thickening and stabilizing the pudding, it needs to be dissolved in cold milk. Otherwise it will clump up and leave your pudding tasting starchy and dry. When you strain the pudding, if you see lots of white clumps in the strainer, it means you didn't mix it enough. You may also wind up with a loose pudding.

Stir Like You Mean It.

Once your pudding is on the heat source, keep it moving—whisk constantly, making sure to reach all the way to the bottom and into the sides of the saucepan with your whisk. If not, the eggs may curdle and a layer of milk may form at the bottom of the saucepan, preventing heat from radiating up into the liquid, posing a risk of the skin being stirred into the pudding.

Look for the Shadow.

At the end of cooking your pudding, press your whisk into the surface of the pudding. The clearer the imprint it leaves when you pick it back up—I call this "the shadow"—the thicker the finished product will be. For the ideal consistency, turn off the heat as soon as you see a faint shadow. Your pudding will appear slightly loose, but it will thicken up further as it chills.

Mind Your Bubbles.

Though the pudding mixture will never come to a full boil, it *will* begin to create big rolling air-pocket bubbles. Once these bubbles begin to form and the pudding begins to thicken, whisk like there's no tomorrow for about 30 seconds, then remove from heat; if you overcook the pudding, it runs the risk of being gritty. The pudding will still seem slightly loose—not as thick as the chilled finished product—and that's just fine.

Be Whole.

For the perfect silky, luxurious texture, I recommend using whole milk and heavy cream for all puddings, but low-fat or even nonfat milk can be substituted. For dairy-free variations, plain or vanilla-flavored coconut or almond milk can be used in place of the milk and cream.

Double Up.

Cooking for a crowd? By all means double or triple the recipes to your heart's content—we certainly do at the shop. Just remember that the more you make, the longer the pudding takes to cook and to cool once finished. If you want the pudding to thicken quickly, cool it in a shallower dish.

Keep Cool and Carry On.

If tightly covered and kept refrigerated, your pudding will stay fresh for four to five days. If you find a little excess liquid pooled at the top after storage, simply drain the liquid off or stir it back into the pudding before serving.

To Skin or Not to Skin?

My pudding recipes call for covering the surface of the semicooled pudding with plastic wrap to avoid developing "pudding skin," a thin layer that forms when pudding is exposed to air. If you're a pudding skin fan, simply omit this step and let the pudding chill uncovered.

SPECIAL EQUIPMENT

One of the best things about the recipes in this book is that they require so little to yield so much. There are only a few pieces of essential equipment that you'll want to have on hand. Unless otherwise noted, all can be found at a kitchen-supply store or large hardware store.

Balloon Whisk: Great for exploring every nook and cranny of a saucepan, a balloon whisk will be your helpmate in keeping the pudding in circulation, preventing clumping and scorching.

Heavy 3-Quart Saucepan: A heavy 3-quart saucepan is ideal for producing a single batch of pudding. If you don't have one, treat yourself; it will help cook the pudding evenly and provide consistent results time after time.

Fine-Mesh Strainer: Once your pudding is cooked, you'll push it through a fine-mesh strainer. This extra step guarantees flawlessly silky pudding.

BASIC INGREDIENTS

Butter

I always recommend using unsalted butter, which allows you to stay in control of how salty you want your desserts to be.

Chocolate

For all recipes calling for 70% cocoa bittersweet chocolate, if possible try to find Nói Síríus brand, which is my hands-down favorite. It can be found in the baking section at Whole Foods markets. The gianduja chocolate called for in the Nutella Pudding can be ordered from Market Hall Foods, www.markethallfoods.com.

Corn Syrup

My motto is "everything in moderation," and that includes corn syrup, which is particularly good for helping create silky sauces. When I call for corn syrup, use light corn syrup, which is milder than the dark variety. If you can find glucose (available at stores like Michael's), feel free to sub that in.

Eggs

Large eggs are the standard for all of my recipes; if you can only find extra large, two extra large eggs equal three large eggs.

Milk

Local, farm-fresh whole milk is the foundation of all of my pudding recipes. While low-fat or nonfat milk can be substituted, whole milk imparts the ideal creaminess. I use milk from Battenkill Valley Creamery, a family-owned dairy farm just a few hours north of New York City.

Salt

Sea salt or plain old table salt should be used in recipes that call for salt, unless kosher salt is specified.

Unsweetened Cocoa

In recipes that call for unsweetened cocoa, both Dutch-processed cocoa, whose acidity has been neutralized with alkali, or the non-alkalized version can be used.

And here we go!

CHAPTER

. . . .

THE
CLASSICS

IF YOU HAD TO MASTER ONE GROUP OF RECIPES IN THIS BOOK, THIS would be it. Basic in technique and elemental in flavor, these recipes will send you straight back to your life's most satisfying dessert moments. What's unique here is the way I achieve my results, generally staying away from extracts and shortcuts and instead favoring an extra step or two—roasting bananas, infusing milk, using only the finest chocolate—that separate these puddings from the pack. Road test these recipes and I think you'll find that rather than being difficult, they're designed to succeed. Most start out similarly: infusing milk with this flavor or that, thickening with cornstarch and eggs, heating into a custard, straining, and cooling. After a while the method becomes second nature, a new dessert language that you'll nearly commit to memory over time.

CHOCOLATE PUDDING · {SERVES 8}

This pudding has major sentimental value, since it was the first one I made for my current business partner, Noah, when I was working as his personal chef. He loved it so much he suggested we open Puddin'—and the rest is history. When we adapted the recipe for the shop, we taste-tested 15 different brands of chocolate, and the clear winner was an Icelandic brand, Noí Sírius. Any other high quality 70 percent cocoa chocolate will do in a pinch. I designed this pudding not to be too sweet or too stiff—I wanted it to have some wiggle to it and allow the purest taste of chocolate to come through.

5 cups whole milk

1 cup heavy cream

3 egg yolks

1 ⅓ cups sugar

¼ cup cocoa powder

¼ cup cornstarch

⅛ teaspoon salt

10 ounces bittersweet chocolate (70% cocoa), finely chopped

1. In a medium saucepan, vigorously whisk together milk, cream, egg yolks, sugar, cocoa powder, cornstarch, and salt.

2. Cook over medium heat, stirring constantly, until warm, 3–4 minutes.

3. Add chocolate and continue to cook, whisking constantly, until pudding begins to thicken, 14–15 minutes. (Once you can lift the whisk from the pudding and it leaves a faint shadow, it's done. The pudding will seem fairly loose, but it will thicken up further as it chills.)

4. Strain the pudding through a fine-mesh sieve into a bowl, pressing pudding through sieve with a silicone spatula.

5. Cool at room temperature for 10 minutes, press a layer of plastic wrap onto the surface of the pudding, and chill until completely cold, 2 hours.

SUGGESTED PAIRING: Whipped Cream (page 66)

VANILLA PUDDING · { SERVES 6-8 }

It may seem like heresy to some, but I love vanilla so much that chocolate comes in a distant second. Growing up, I got in the habit of dabbing my mom's Madagascar vanilla extract behind my ears, and it quickly became my signature scent. I usually avoid using flavor extracts in my recipes, but this one is an exception—the round, floral, and musky notes of good-quality vanilla extract reinforce the flavor achieved by infusing the milk and cream with a scraped vanilla bean. And you can forget about vanilla's reputation for being "boring"—even sworn chocoholics are converted once they taste this version. One spoonful of this pure, simple treat, and you'll see why.

2 ½ cups whole milk

2 ½ cups heavy cream

1 vanilla bean, split, seeds scraped out and reserved

1 cup sugar

6 tablespoons cornstarch

6 egg yolks

¼ teaspoon salt

2 teaspoons vanilla extract

1. In a medium saucepan heat the milk, cream, and vanilla bean and seeds until steaming but not boiling. Remove from heat and allow to steep 30 minutes. Chill completely in refrigerator, 1–2 hours.

2. Add sugar, cornstarch, egg yolks, and salt to saucepan and whisk vigorously.

3. Place pot over medium-high heat and cook, whisking constantly, until mixture begins to thicken, 5–6 minutes. (Once you can lift the whisk from the pudding and it leaves a faint shadow, it's done. Pudding will seem fairly loose, but it will thicken up further as it chills.)

4. Strain the pudding through a fine-mesh sieve into a bowl, pressing pudding through sieve with a silicone spatula. Whisk in vanilla extract.

5. Cool at room temperature for 10 minutes, press a layer of plastic wrap onto the surface of the pudding, and chill completely in refrigerator, 2 hours.

SUGGESTED PAIRINGS: Salted Caramel Sauce (page 58); Fudge Sauce (page 61); Cherry Compote (page 63)

BUTTERSCOTCH PUDDING · { SERVES 8 }

Ever since I was a kid, my dad's nightly indulgence has been a single glass of Famous Grouse Scotch whiskey, which he nurses throughout the night. When I started rethinking butterscotch pudding, I used that ice-filled glass with its slowly receding contents as my inspiration—and Dad's bottle of hooch as "research material." Then I had some fun by cooking up some brown butter, which adds a roasty, toasty, nutty flavor that makes everything it touches taste a little bit better. I add the shot of dad's Famous Grouse at the end for maximum impact. Dad, this one's for you—I promise to replace that bottle sometime soon!

FOR THE BUTTERSCOTCH SAUCE:

1 stick butter

½ cup heavy cream

1 cup loosely packed dark
   brown sugar

1 teaspoon salt

4 teaspoons vanilla extract

FOR THE PUDDING:

2 ½ cups whole milk

2 ½ cups heavy cream

6 tablespoons cornstarch

2 tablespoons dark brown sugar

¼ teaspoon salt

6 egg yolks

2 teaspoons vanilla extract

2–3 tablespoons Scotch whiskey
   (preferably Famous Grouse; amount
   depends on how strong you want it)

MAKE BUTTERSCOTCH SAUCE:

1. Melt butter in a small saucepan over medium heat, cooking until golden brown in color, 2–3 minutes. The butter should look like honey and smell like freshly baked chocolate chip cookies.

2. Add cream, brown sugar, and salt, then raise heat to medium high and bring to

CONTINUED

a boil. Cook, stirring, until sugar is dissolved and mixture is thickened, 4–5 minutes.

3. Remove from heat, stir in vanilla, cover, and set aside.

MAKE PUDDING:

1. In a medium saucepan, vigorously whisk together milk, cream, cornstarch, brown sugar, salt, and egg yolks.

2. Cook over medium-high heat, whisking constantly, until mixture is thickened, 6–8 minutes. (Once you can lift the whisk from the pudding and it leaves a faint shadow, it's done.)

3. Strain the pudding through a fine-mesh sieve into a bowl, pressing pudding through sieve with a silicone spatula. Whisk in vanilla and scotch.

4. Pour the warm butterscotch sauce into the hot pudding base in three additions, whisking until fully incorporated.

5. Cool at room temperature for 10 minutes, press a layer of plastic wrap onto the surface of the pudding, and chill completely in refrigerator, 2 hours.

SUGGESTED PAIRINGS: Peanut Brittle Bits (page 69); Salted Caramel Sauce (page 58)

Butterscotch Pudding
with Salted Caramel Sauce
(pages 5 and 58)

BANANA PUDDING · { SERVES 6-8 }

There's definitely a banana divide in my family. My mom, the banana-hater, sits on one side of the fence, while the rest of us sit on the other, peeling to our hearts' content. Me? I love banana shakes, banana cake, banana ice cream—you name it! Creating this pudding, I knew I didn't want to use banana extract or banana liqueur, so I had my work cut out for me. Mom and I discovered a method of roasting bananas whole in their skins; the bananas turn soft and gray on the outside, almost caramelizing. After roasting, let them cool for a while—no one wants to peel a hot banana!

8 ripe medium bananas, skins on (about 3 ½–4 pounds)

2 ½ cups whole milk

2 ½ cups heavy cream

1 cup sugar

6 tablespoons cornstarch

6 egg yolks

¼ teaspoon salt

1. Preheat oven to 350°F.

2. Place bananas (do not peel) on a rimmed baking sheet and poke all over with a fork. (Go ahead—just let all your rage out on those bananas.)

3. Roast bananas until super-soft, 25–30 minutes. Let cool at room temperature for 20 minutes.

4. In a medium saucepan over medium-high heat, heat milk and cream until hot to the touch but not boiling, about 7–8 minutes. Remove saucepan from heat.

5. Peel bananas and mash in a bowl, add to hot milk, cool at room temperature for 15 minutes, and cover. Let steep in refrigerator at least 4 hours and up to 24 hours.

6. Over a medium saucepan, pour bananas and milk through a fine-mesh strainer or wrap in a double layer of cheesecloth. Strain as much of the milk out of the bananas as you can, reserving banana mash for Banana Upside-Down Cake with Malted Pudding (page 91).

7. Add sugar, cornstarch, egg yolks, and salt to saucepan and whisk thoroughly. Cook over medium heat, whisking constantly, until mixture begins to thicken, 9 minutes. (Once you can lift the whisk from the pudding and it leaves a faint shadow, it's done. Pudding will seem fairly loose, but it will thicken up further as it chills.)

8. Strain the pudding through a fine-mesh strainer into a bowl, pressing pudding through sieve with a silicone spatula.

9. Cool at room temperature for 10 minutes, press a layer of plastic wrap onto the surface of the pudding, and chill completely in refrigerator, 2 hours.

SUGGESTED PAIRING: Whipped Cream (page 66) and Vanilla Wafers (page 57)

COFFEE PUDDING · {SERVES 6}

"We've never seen you drink so much coffee," my friends have told me since I opened Puddin', and it's true. The long hours and often crazy-early start times have converted me into a java monster. So when people ask me about my favorite flavor, I always tell them it's this one, which I developed to taste like the perfect sip of espresso. There are lots of instant espresso powders out there, but by far my favorite is Medaglia d'Oro, which is widely available and contains more natural oils that help impart a direct hit of coffee goodness into every bite. Your taste buds first notice a touch of bitterness, followed by nutty and creamy notes—and the perfect off-sweet finish.

2 cups heavy cream

2 cups whole milk

$\frac{1}{2}$ cup plus 2 tablespoons light brown sugar

3 tablespoons instant espresso powder

3 tablespoons cornstarch

1 egg yolk

$\frac{1}{2}$ teaspoon salt

1. In a medium saucepan whisk together all ingredients.

2. Cook over medium-high heat, whisking constantly, until mixture begins to thicken, 10–12 minutes. (Once you can lift the whisk from the pudding and it leaves a faint shadow, it's done. Pudding will seem fairly loose, but it will thicken up further as it chills.)

3. Strain the pudding through a fine-mesh sieve into a bowl, pressing pudding through sieve with a silicone spatula.

4. Cool at room temperature for 10 minutes, press a layer of plastic wrap onto the surface of the pudding, and chill completely in refrigerator, 2 hours.

SUGGESTED PAIRINGS: Salted Caramel Sauce (page 58); Fudge Sauce (page 61); Brownie Crumbs (page 49)

HEVRA'S LEMON OBSESSION PUDDING · { SERVES 6-8 }

There were no lemon trees in our suburban Ohio backyard, but there might as well have been, what with the number of lemons in our kitchen when I was a kid. My mom, Hevra, is lemon-obsessed, and never met a recipe she didn't think could be improved by a squeeze of zesty, tangy citrus. To her, heaven is a jar of fresh lemon curd, which became the inspiration for this recipe. I wanted something meltier and a bit less tart than straight lemon curd, so my mom and I came up with the idea of stirring a homemade curd into a pudding base at the end of cooking. Because there's butter in the curd, this pudding definitely has a richer, rounder flavor than some of the others. Mom, this one's for you.

1 ¼ cups whole milk

1 ¼ cups heavy cream

¼ cup sugar

3 tablespoons cornstarch

3 egg yolks

⅛ teaspoon salt

1 ½ cups Lemon Curd (see page 12)

1. Make curd (see page 12).

2. In a medium saucepan vigorously whisk together the milk, cream, sugar, cornstarch, egg yolks, and salt.

3. Cook over medium-high heat, whisking constantly, until thick, 5-6 minutes. (Once you can lift the whisk from the pudding and it leaves a faint shadow, it's done.)

4. Strain the pudding through a fine-mesh sieve into a bowl, pressing pudding through sieve with a silicone spatula.

5. Cool at room temperature for 10 minutes, press a layer of plastic wrap onto the surface of the pudding, and chill until completely cold, 2 hours.

6. When the curd and pudding are chilled, in a medium bowl whisk them together until well blended.

SUGGESTED PAIRINGS: Lime Angel Food Cake Crumbs (page 48); Blackberry Compote (page 63), Marshmallow Crème (page 67)

LEMON CURD ·

This curd is an essential ingredient in both Hevra's Lemon Obsession Pudding (page 11) and our Lemon Lover's Cake (page 99). It's also great dolloped onto fresh fruit, over pound cake, or even stirred into a bowl of Greek yogurt.

½ cup plus 2 tablespoons lemon juice (about 3 lemons' worth)

2 eggs

2 egg yolks

½ cup sugar

⅛ teaspoon salt

Finely grated zest of 1 lemon

5 tablespoons butter, melted

1. In a small saucepan combine all ingredients except butter, then drizzle in butter and whisk constantly over medium heat until curd begins to coat the back of a spoon, 3–4 minutes.

2. Strain the curd through a fine-mesh sieve into a bowl, pressing curd through sieve with a silicone spatula.

3. Cool 5 minutes, then press a layer of plastic wrap onto the surface of the curd and chill completely in refrigerator, 1 hour.

NOTE: This recipe works beautifully with grapefruit juice, too. The only catch is that you have to reduce a larger quantity of juice to achieve the proper tartness necessary to make the pudding's flavor really pop. To do so, in a small saucepan boil 3 cups fresh grapefruit juice over medium-high heat until reduced to ½ cup, about 20 minutes. Cool completely at room temperature before using.

APRICOT-SCENTED RICE PUDDING · { SERVES 8 }

I've loved the flavor of rice pudding for as long as I can remember, but I often find that overcooked rice turns this classic into a major bummer. The solution came to me one day at an Indian restaurant while I was spooning raita, the traditional savory Indian yogurt sauce, onto my rice. I was struck by the way the firm, perfectly cooked grain was enhanced but not overtaken by the creamy yogurt. Then it hit me: why couldn't I make rice pudding like this? I cooked the rice in milk then made a separate pudding and stirred the two together. You get firm rice, creamy custard, and a subtle apricot flavor.

FOR THE APRICOT SYRUP:

½ cup sugar

12 dried apricots, diced (½ cup)

FOR THE RICE:

¾ cup long-grain basmati rice

1 ⅓ cups whole milk

4 tablespoons Apricot Syrup (without solids)

¼ teaspoon salt

FOR THE PUDDING:

1 ¾ cups whole milk

1 ¾ cups heavy cream

1 cinnamon stick

1 vanilla bean, split, seeds scraped out and reserved

¾ cup sugar

4½ tablespoons cornstarch

4 egg yolks

MAKE APRICOT SYRUP:

1. Bring ½ cup water and the sugar to a boil in a small saucepan.

2. Remove from heat, add the apricots, and transfer to a bowl to cool at room temperature. (The syrup is ready to use right away, but the longer you leave in the apricots, the more apricot-a-licious the syrup will be.) Reserve syrup and solids.

CONTINUED

1. Preheat the oven to 300°F.

2. In a small, ovenproof saucepan bring the rice and 2 cups cold water to a boil. Immediately remove from heat, drain, and rinse the rice right away under fresh cold water. Drain rice in a fine-mesh seive.

3. Return the rice to the same pot and add the milk, apricot syrup, and salt.

4. Cover the pot with a tight-fitting lid, transfer the pot to the oven, and cook, stirring every 10 minutes, until the milk is completely absorbed and the rice is plump, 45 minutes.

5. Remove pot from oven and let stand, covered, for at least 15 minutes.

MAKE PUDDING:

1. In a medium saucepan whisk together the milk and cream, then add the cinnamon stick and vanilla bean. Heat the mixture gently until hot but not boiling, 5 minutes, remove from heat, and let steep, covered, until milk comes to room temperature, 20 minutes. Chill in refrigerator for at least 10 minutes.

2. Add sugar, cornstarch, and egg yolks to chilled milk mixture and whisk vigorously.

3. Return the saucepan to the stovetop and cook over medium-high heat, whisking constantly, until mixture is thick, 5–6 minutes. (Once you can lift the whisk from the pudding and it leaves a faint shadow, it's done.)

4. Strain the pudding through a fine-mesh strainer into a bowl, pressing pudding through sieve with a silicone spatula. Remove vanilla bean and cinnamon stick and discard. Fold rice and reserved apricots into hot custard.

5. Cover surface of pudding with plastic wrap, cool 10 minutes, then chill in refrigerator until completely cold, 2 hours.

SUGGESTED PAIRING: Cherry Compote (page 66)

Apricot Scented Rice Pudding

TAPIOCA PUDDING · {SERVES 6}

I've always wanted to be on the tapioca pudding train, but this classic desert can feel a little humdrum to me. Traditionally, those tiny, dried tapioca pearls, which are made from the starchy manioc root, are rehydrated with water, milk, and cream to form a rich pudding. By switching it up with a combination of milk and canned sweetened condensed milk, I achieved a gorgeous pudding that doesn't compromise tapioca's unique, squidgy texture while adding an incredible sweet and milky twist.

½ cup small pearl tapioca

1 egg

1 egg yolk

One 14-ounce can sweetened condensed milk, divided

1 ½ cups whole milk

Finely grated zest of half a lemon

1 teaspoon vanilla extract

⅛ teaspoon salt

1. Soak tapioca pearls in 2 cups cold water in refrigerator for at least 2 hours or overnight; drain tapioca but don't rinse.

2. In the bowl of a stand mixer fitted with the whisk attachment, beat the egg, egg yolk, and ⅓ cup sweetened condensed milk on high speed, 2–3 minutes.

3. In a medium saucepan combine the tapioca, remaining sweetened condensed milk, and milk. Bring mixture to a low boil, stirring constantly with a silicone spatula, then reduce heat to a simmer and cook until tapioca pearls are clear and the mixture is somewhat thickened, 9–10 minutes total. Remove from heat.

4. Return mixer to medium speed and add ½ cup of the hot tapioca mixture into the whipped egg and condensed milk mixture to temper it; whip until mixture is warm, 10 seconds. Gradually pour the tempered egg mixture into the saucepan, whisking constantly.

5. Whisk mixture over low heat until thickened and custardlike, about 1 minute; do not overcook or the eggs may curdle. Stir in lemon zest, vanilla, and salt.

6. Cool at room temperature for 10 minutes, press a layer of plastic wrap onto the surface of the pudding, and chill completely in refrigerator, 2 hours.

HAPPENS-TO-BE-VEGAN
COCONUT PUDDING · { SERVES 4-6 }

You have to try this coconut pudding to believe it—it's so creamy, lush, and delicate that everyone thinks it has eggs, milk, and cream in it like most of its pudding siblings. But this one is happily, naturally vegan—just some coconut milk bound with enough sugar and cornstarch to enhance, but not overpower, its tropical goodness. Some recipes survive a low-fat swap-in, but this isn't one of them; go for the gusto with rich full-fat coconut milk, and you may become a vegan yourself! This is a great pudding to pair with fresh fruit. Try it with ripe mango, pineapple, or berries.

3 ¾ cups (two 13 ½-ounce cans) unsweetened full-fat coconut milk

½ cup sugar

5 tablespoons cornstarch

¼ teaspoon salt

1. In a medium saucepan vigorously whisk together all ingredients.

2. Cook over medium-high heat, whisking constantly, until mixture is thickened, 8–9 minutes. (Once you can lift the whisk from the pudding and it leaves a faint shadow, it's done.)

3. Strain the pudding through a fine-mesh sieve into a bowl, pressing pudding through sieve with a silicone spatula. Cool at room temperature for 10 minutes, press a layer of plastic wrap onto the surface of the pudding, and chill completely in refrigerator, 2 hours.

NOTE: If pudding is very stiff after chilling, add ½ cup additional coconut milk and beat on high in a stand mixer or with an electric hand mixer until smooth and creamy, 1–2 minutes.

SUGGESTED PAIRINGS: Fresh fruit; Cherry Compote (page 63); Vegan Fudge Sauce (page 61)

CHAPTER

. . . .

NEW FAVORITES

CREATING THESE RECIPES WAS A BLAST FOR ME, ALLOWING ME TO TRANSLATE many of my favorite flavors and taste memories into distinctive deserts. This group of recipes also allowed me to put my professional pastry kitchen experience to good use. You'll find tart citrus curds stirred into the Key lime and passion fruit puddings, a yolk-infused base in the Boston Cream pudding, and scraped vanilla beans in many recipes. At the shop, we rotate these flavors based on the season, customer requests, or a simple desire to introduce something unique. Have fun experimenting and discovering your own favorites.

NUTELLA PUDDING · {SERVES 6}

The Italians are responsible for lots of great things in this world, among them the Sistine Chapel, Fellini films, and gnocchi. Right up there on the list is Nutella. I love the stuff so much that no matter where I am, a jar of it is bound to be perched somewhere in the vicinity. My mom and I collaborated on this Nutella-inspired recipe, which uses a combination of hazelnut-steeped milk, cocoa powder, and gianduja chocolate bars to replicate an ingredient with a cult following.

2 cups whole milk

1 cup half-and-half

1 1/2 cups roasted and peeled hazelnuts, roughly chopped

3 egg yolks

1/3 cup light brown sugar

3 tablespoons cornstarch

2 tablespoons granulated sugar

2 tablespoons cocoa powder

2 teaspoons instant espresso powder

1/8 teaspoon salt

6 ounces dark gianduja chocolate, finely chopped

1 teaspoon vanilla extract

1. Heat the milk and half-and-half in a saucepan over medium-high heat until steaming but not boiling, 5 minutes.

2. Place the hazelnuts in a medium heatproof bowl and pour the hot milk mixture over the nuts. Cool until the mixture reaches room temperature, 30 minutes, then cover and refrigerate at least 4 hours and up to 24 hours.

3. Strain the milk into a large measuring cup, reserving the hazelnuts for another use, such as Hazelnut Crepe Cake (page 118). If needed, add additional milk to total 3 cups of liquid.

4. In a medium saucepan vigorously whisk together the hazelnut milk, egg yolks, brown sugar, cornstarch, sugar, cocoa powder, espresso powder, and salt.

CONTINUED

5. Add the gianduja and cook over medium-high heat, whisking constantly, until pudding begins to thicken, 4–5 minutes. (Once you can lift the whisk from the pudding and it leaves a faint shadow, it's done. Pudding will seem fairly loose, but it will thicken up further as it chills.) Remove from heat and whisk in vanilla.

6. Strain the pudding through a fine-mesh sieve into a bowl, pressing pudding through sieve with a spatula.

7. Cool at room temperature for 10 minutes, press a layer of plastic wrap onto the surface of the pudding, and chill completely cold in refrigerator, 2 hours.

SUGGESTED PAIRINGS: Caramel Whipped Cream (page 66); Candied Mixed Nuts (page 68); Peanut Brittle Bits (page 69)

PEANUT BUTTER PUDDING

{ SERVES 6-8 }

During the recipe-testing phase for the shop, a good friend requested a peanut butter pudding cake for her birthday. Who was I to refuse her? The resulting cake was so popular, it—and the pudding that inspired it—just had to stay on the store's menu. While natural-style peanut butter rocks on toast, on fresh bananas, and just about every other way, this recipe demands creamy, commercial peanut butter—it makes for a smoother finished product.

3 1/4 cups whole milk

1 cup heavy cream

1 1/2 cups smooth peanut butter (preferably not natural)

3/4 cup sugar

1/4 cup cornstarch

1 teaspoon salt

1. In a medium saucepan vigorously whisk together all of the ingredients until smooth.

2. Cook over medium-high heat, whisking constantly, until mixture begins to thicken, 7–8 minutes. (Once you can lift the whisk from the pudding and it leaves a faint shadow, it's done. Pudding will seem fairly loose, but it will thicken up further as it chills.)

3. Strain the pudding through a fine-mesh sieve into a bowl, pressing pudding through sieve with a spatula.

4. Cool at room temperature for 10 minutes, press a layer of plastic wrap onto the surface of the pudding, and chill completely in refrigerator, 2 hours.

SUGGESTED PAIRINGS: Fudge Sauce (page 61); Chocowich Bits (page 50); Marshmallow Crème (page 67)

Vegan Peanut Butter Pudding

BECAUSE THIS RECIPE doesn't contain any eggs, it can easily be made vegan. For vegan peanut butter pudding, use unsweetened almond milk (4 1/4 cups) in place of the milk and heavy cream.

DULCE DE LECHE PUDDING · { SERVES 6 }

I've loved dulce de leche—technically translated as "milk candy"—for as long as I can remember. Its deep, butterscotch-caramel flavor is a staple in Central and South American countries, where it's layered between sandwich cookies, made into individual candies, and even spread on bread. Here, the flavor stars in a crazy-good pudding. I challenge you to try to avoid eating the whole batch at once, spoonful by spoonful—it is that dangerously delicious.

1¼ cups whole milk

1¼ cups heavy cream

6 tablespoons cornstarch

3 egg yolks

1 tablespoon dark brown sugar

⅛ teaspoon salt

2 recipes Dulce de Leche (page 62), or 3 cups store-bought dulce de leche, warm

1. In a medium saucepan vigorously whisk together the milk, heavy cream, cornstarch, egg yolks, brown sugar, and salt.

2. Cook over medium-high heat, whisking constantly, until thick, 5–6 minutes. (Once you can lift the whisk from the pudding and it leaves a faint shadow, it's done; this pudding will seem much thicker than others, but once you add the sauce it will thin out.)

3. Strain the pudding through a fine-mesh sieve into a bowl, pressing pudding through sieve with a silicone spatula.

4. Whisk the dulce de leche directly into the hot pudding base until fully incorporated.

5. Cool at room temperature for 10 minutes, press a layer of plastic wrap onto the surface of the pudding, and chill completely in refrigerator, 2 hours.

SUGGESTED PAIRINGS: Very Vanilla Cake crumbs (see note page 112); Vanilla Wafers (page 57)

MY BRO'S MALTED MILK PUDDING • { SERVES 4-6 }

This recipe is time-stamped to my brother Emmett's malted-milkshake period, circa 2011, which, if we're being honest, lasted for more than a little while. I was temporarily living with my parents at the time, and I remember waking up to the entire house infused with the toasty-sweet aroma of malt. So I went to work making malted milk pudding, which has become quite a favorite in the shop. Original malted milk powder is my default ingredient here, but you can also use the chocolate version if you're feeling adventurous.

1 ¼ cups whole milk

1 ¼ cups heavy cream

½ teaspoon salt

½ cup sugar

3 tablespoons cornstarch

3 egg yolks

1 cup plus 2 tablespoons malted milk powder

1 ounce bittersweet chocolate, finely chopped

1 teaspoon vanilla extract

1. In a medium saucepan vigorously whisk together all ingredients except vanilla.

2. Cook over medium-high heat, whisking constantly, until thick, 6–7 minutes. (Once you can lift the whisk from the pudding and it leaves a faint shadow, it's done.) Whisk in vanilla.

3. Strain the pudding through a fine-mesh sieve into a bowl, pressing pudding through sieve with a spatula.

4. Cool at room temperature for 10 minutes, press a layer of plastic wrap onto the surface of the pudding, and chill completely in a refrigerator, 2 hours.

SUGGESTED PAIRINGS: Chocowich Bits (page 50); Banana Upside-Down Cake Crumbs (see note page 112)

BOSTON CREAM PUDDING · { SERVES 6-8 }

Designed as a component of my Boston Cream Pie (page 109), this extra-eggy pudding is richness personified. If you're choosing to steal a cupful on its own, try pairing it with a tart compote, such as our Cranberry, Orange, and Ginger Compote (page 64), for contrast.

2 ½ cups whole milk

2 ½ cups heavy cream

¾ cup sugar

5 tablespoons cornstarch

6 egg yolks

¼ teaspoon salt

1 tablespoon vanilla extract

1. In a medium saucepan whisk together all ingredients except vanilla.

3. Cook over medium-high heat, whisking constantly, until mixture begins to thicken, 5–6 minutes. (Once you can lift the whisk from the pudding and it leaves a faint shadow, it's done. Pudding will seem fairly loose, but it will thicken up further as it chills.)

4. Strain the pudding through a fine-mesh sieve into a bowl, pressing pudding through sieve with a silicone spatula. Whisk in vanilla.

5. Cool at room temperature for 10 minutes, press a layer of plastic wrap onto the surface of the pudding, and chill completely in refrigerator, 2 hours.

SUGGESTED PAIRINGS: Cranberry, Orange, and Ginger Compote (page 64); Fudge Sauce (page 61)

ROASTED CASHEW PUDDING · { SERVES 6 }

I have food cravings almost as often as I breathe, and cashews are a frequent one. When I developed this pudding I was going through a particularly profound cashew fixation; I would have eaten an old sock if it had cashews in it! This recipe came out of that obsession, when I discovered that cashews are absolutely perfect for pudding. They're the richest, most luxurious, most luscious nut I can think of, with a flavor that calls to mind a crock of butter infused with just a subtle touch of fragile nuttiness. After you roast the cashews, don't wait for them to cool down; chopping them quickly and getting them into the hot milk while still warm helps release their magically flavorful oils.

2 cups whole raw cashews

1 1/4 cups whole milk

1 1/4 cups heavy cream

1/2 cup sugar

3 tablespoons cornstarch

3 egg yolks

1/8 teaspoon salt

1. Preheat oven to 350°F.

2. Place cashews on a rimmed baking sheet and roast until lightly golden and fragrant, 7–8 minutes.

3. Place the hot cashews in a food processor and pulse until roughly chopped, 3–4 pulses (warning: do not overpulse or you'll be dealing with cashew paste), or place in a towel and smash with a rolling pin or wine bottle.

4. In a medium saucepan heat the milk, cream, and chopped cashews until steaming but not boiling, 5–6 minutes. Steep in the refrigerator for a minimum of 2 hours; for maximum cashewness, steep overnight.

5. Strain the milk into a large measuring cup and discard cashews. If needed, add additional milk to total 2 1/2 cups liquid.

6. In a medium saucepan combine strained cashew milk with remaining ingredients and whisk vigorously.

CONTINUED

7. Cook over medium-high heat, whisking constantly, until mixture begins to thicken, 5–6 minutes. (Once you can lift the whisk from the pudding and it leaves a faint shadow, it's done. Pudding will seem fairly loose, but it will thicken up further as it chills.)

8. Strain the pudding through a fine-mesh sieve into a bowl, pressing pudding through sieve with a spatula.

9. Cool at room temperature for 10 minutes, press a layer of plastic wrap onto the surface of the pudding, and chill completely in refrigerator, 2 hours.

SUGGESTED PAIRING: **Candied Mixed Nuts (page 68)**

DESPERATE MEASURES MINT CHIP PUDDING · { SERVES 6 }

I'm a diehard mint lover, and I can trace the roots of my mint obsession back to my native Buckeye State of Ohio. Back in Cleveland there exists a magical ice cream company called Pierre's, whose mint chocolate chip scoop contains thin chocolate shards rather than those pesky chocolate chips that freeze up, get hard, and can potentially chip your dental fillings. Coming to New York and discovering the glaring lack of Pierre's brought me a newfound understanding of a phrase I'd heard my whole life: "Desperate times call for desperate measures." So after I realized that I was always loading up my standard mint pudding recipe with chocolate sprinkles, I let this recipe succumb to the lure of a Pierre's-style confection.

1 ¼ cups whole milk

1 ¼ cups heavy cream

1 small bunch fresh mint, rinsed and dried

¼ cup sugar

3 tablespoons cornstarch

3 egg yolks

⅛ teaspoon salt

4 ounces bittersweet chocolate (70% cocoa), chopped

1. In a medium saucepan heat milk and cream over medium heat until very hot but not boiling, 4–5 minutes. Add mint, remove from heat, and let steep until cooled to room temperature, 20–30 minutes, then chill overnight or up to 24 hours in refrigerator.

2. Strain milk and return to saucepan, discarding mint. Add the sugar, cornstarch, egg yolks, and salt, and whisk vigorously.

3. Cook over medium-high heat, whisking constantly, until mixture begins to thicken, 5–6 minutes. (Once you can lift the whisk from the pudding and it leaves a faint shadow, it's done. Pudding will seem fairly loose, but it will thicken up further as it chills.)

4. Strain the pudding through a fine-mesh sieve into a bowl, pressing pudding through sieve with a spatula.

5. Cool at room temperature for 10 minutes, press a layer of plastic wrap onto the surface of the pudding, and chill completely in refrigerator, 2 hours.

CONTINUED

6.   Line a 9-by-9-inch square pan with parchment paper and set aside. In a double boiler melt chocolate until smooth. Pour into prepared parchment-lined pan and freeze until you've got one paper-thin, solid piece of chocolate, 15–20 minutes.

7.   Using your hands, break up chocolate into shards and stir into the chilled pudding until it looks like a Jackson Pollock painting.

SUGGESTED PAIRING: **Brownie Crumbs (page 49)**

PASSION FRUIT PUDDING · {SERVES 6-8}

During my time in the kitchen at Daniel Boulud's DB Bistro Moderne, one of the desserts I had the privilege of making was a tart fruit crémeux with hazelnut mousse and macarons. The dessert was tangy yet light, and I knew I had to convey that taste experience in a pudding. The result is this tart and rich passion fruit pudding. Look for juice that is as pure and concentrated as you can find—the better the curd, the better the pudding!

FOR THE CURD:

½ cup plus 2 tablespoons pure passion fruit puree (available at specialty stores)

2 tablespoons lemon juice

2 eggs

2 egg yolks

5 tablespoons butter, melted

½ cup sugar

⅛ teaspoon salt

Zest from 1 lemon

FOR THE PUDDING:

1 ¼ cups milk

1 ¼ cups heavy cream

¼ cup sugar

3 tablespoons cornstarch

3 egg yolks

⅛ teaspoon salt

1 teaspoon vanilla extract

MAKE CURD:

1. In a small saucepan combine all ingredients and whisk constantly over medium heat until curd coats back of spoon, 6–7 minutes. (Curd will seem fairly loose.)

2. Strain the curd through a fine-mesh sieve into a bowl, pressing curd through sieve with a silicone spatula.

3. Press a layer of plastic wrap onto the surface of the curd and chill until completely cold, 1 hour.

CONTINUED

MAKE PUDDING:

1. In a medium saucepan vigorously whisk together all ingredients except vanilla.

2. Cook over medium-high heat, whisking constantly, until mixture is thick, 5–6 minutes. (Once you can lift the whisk from the pudding and it leaves a shadow, it's done.)

3. Strain the pudding through a fine-mesh sieve into a bowl, pressing pudding through sieve with a silicone spatula. Whisk in vanilla.

4. Cool at room temperature for 10 minutes, press a layer of plastic wrap onto the surface of the pudding, and chill completely in refrigerator, 2 hours.

5. When the curd and the pudding are chilled, in a medium bowl whisk them together until incorporated.

PINEAPPLE PUDDING · {SERVES 6-8}

I don't drink alcohol (trust me, I don't need it), but I like to have a drink in hand when everyone else is celebrating with a cocktail. My choice is always a virgin piña colada—that combination of creamy and fruity, with tropical notes, gets me every time. When I got to thinking about translating those flavors into a pudding, I realized I was onto something. Here, pineapple curd gets stirred into a pudding that's ultra-creamy, with a resulting flavor that reminds me of a pineapple Creamsicle.

FOR THE CURD:

- 3 cups fresh or canned pineapple juice
- 2 tablespoons lemon juice
- 2 eggs
- 2 egg yolks
- 5 tablespoons butter, melted
- 1/2 cup sugar
- 1/8 teaspoon salt
- Zest from 1 lemon

FOR THE PUDDING:

- 1 1/4 cups whole milk
- 1 1/4 cups heavy cream
- 1/4 cup sugar
- 3 tablespoons cornstarch
- 3 egg yolks
- 1/8 teaspoon salt

MAKE CURD:

1. In a small saucepan bring the pineapple juice to a boil over medium-high heat and cook until the juice is reduced to 1/2 cup, 20 minutes.

2. Add remaining ingredients and cook, stirring, over medium heat until curd coats spoon, 6–7 minutes.

3. Strain the curd through a fine-mesh sieve into a bowl, pressing curd through sieve with a spatula.

CONTINUED

4. Press a layer of plastic wrap onto the surface of the curd and chill completely in refrigerator, 2 hours.

MAKE PUDDING:

1. In a medium saucepan combine all ingredients and whisk vigorously.

2. Cook over medium-high heat, whisking constantly, until mixture is thick, 5–6 minutes. (Once you can lift the whisk from the pudding and it leaves a shadow, it's done.)

3. Strain the pudding through a fine-mesh sieve into a bowl, pressing pudding through sieve with a silicone spatula.

4. Cool at room temperature for 10 minutes, press a layer of plastic wrap onto the surface of the pudding, and chill completely in refrigerator, 2 hours.

5. When the curd and the pudding are chilled, in a medium bowl whisk them together until well blended.

SUGGESTED PAIRINGS: **Candied Mixed Nuts (page 68);**
Marshmallow Crème (page 67)

KEY LIME PUDDING · { SERVES 6 }

This pudding was created in the service of one of the shop's most popular desserts—a Key lime pudding cheesecake. Even non-sweets people (do they *really* exist?) like this one, owing to its pleasingly pucker-inducing sourness. Tiny and tart, Key limes have a super-acidic but also slightly more floral flavor than plain old limes, which are known as Persian limes. Try to get fresh Key limes for this—they often come in a net bag since they're so little—and use a clamp-style citrus squeezer to extract the juice from the little green spheres. If you can't find them, bottled Key lime juice is available in many stores. You can also use regular limes in a pinch.

FOR THE CURD:

1/2 cup plus 2 tablespoons Key lime juice or regular lime juice

2 eggs

2 egg yolks

5 tablespoons butter, melted

1/2 cup sugar

1/8 teaspoon salt

Zest from 3 Key limes or 1 regular lime

FOR THE PUDDING:

1 1/4 cups whole milk

1 1/4 cups heavy cream

1/4 cup sugar

3 tablespoons cornstarch

1/8 teaspoon salt

3 egg yolks

1 teaspoon vanilla extract

MAKE CURD:

1. In a small saucepan combine all ingredients and whisk constantly over medium heat until curd coats the back of a spoon, 4–5 minutes.

2. Strain the curd through a fine-mesh sieve into a bowl, pressing curd through sieve with a spatula.

CONTINUED

3. Press a layer of plastic wrap onto the surface of the curd and chill completely in refrigerator, 1 hour.

MAKE PUDDING:

1. In a medium saucepan combine all ingredients except vanilla and whisk vigorously until smooth.

2. Cook over medium-high heat, whisking constantly, until thick, 5–6 minutes. (Once you can lift the whisk from the pudding and it leaves a shadow, it's done.)

3. Strain the pudding through a fine-mesh sieve into a bowl, pressing pudding through sieve with a spatula. Whisk in vanilla.

4. Cool at room temperature for 10 minutes, press a layer of plastic wrap onto the surface of the pudding, and chill completely in refrigerator, 2 hours.

5. When the curd and pudding are chilled, in a medium bowl whisk them together until well blended.

SUGGESTED PAIRING: Graham Crumbs (page 56) and
Whipped Cream (page 66)

MAPLE PUDDING · { SERVES 4-6 }

I spend most of my waking hours at Puddin', in the company of a great staff who turn what could just be a job into a close community. Inevitably someone gets a crazy food craving, and it's in my nature to try to satisfy it. One night, after thirteen hours stirring pudding, one of my employees expressed a craving for pancakes and syrup. Next thing I knew, the neurons in my pudding-centric brain began to fire, and zing!—maple pudding was born. For this recipe try to use dark, intense grade B maple syrup, with its incredibly complex flavor. Stirring it in toward the end ensures that you'll be able to detect all of the syrup's subtlties. Make sure to add the syrup slowly; adding it too fast could cause your pudding to become liquidy.

1¼ cups whole milk

1¼ cups heavy cream

6 tablespoons cornstarch

3 egg yolks

¼ cup dark brown sugar

⅛ teaspoon salt

1 teaspoon vanilla extract

1 cup good-quality maple syrup, preferably grade B

1. In a medium saucepan vigorously whisk together the milk, cream, cornstarch, egg yolks, brown sugar, and salt.

2. Cook over medium heat, whisking constantly, until the mixture is thick, 5–6 minutes. (Once you can lift the whisk from the pudding and it leaves a shadow, it's done; this pudding will seem much thicker than others, but once you add the maple syrup it will thin out.)

3. Strain the pudding through a fine-mesh sieve into a bowl, pressing pudding through sieve with a spatula. Whisk in vanilla, then slowly whisk in maple syrup.

4. Cool at room temperature for 10 minutes, press a layer of plastic wrap onto the surface of the pudding, and chill completely in refrigerator, 2 hours.

SUGGESTED PAIRING: Maple-Apple Topping (page 65)

PUMPKIN PIE PUDDING · {SERVES 6}

Roasted, stuffed, baked, sweet, savory—no matter how it's served, I just love pumpkin! The inspiration for this recipe came one Thanksgiving a few years back when I was celebrating the holiday with my family and some friends. I wanted to take my passion for pumpkin and turn it into something special, so I made a pudding that mimicked pumpkin pie in all of the best ways—the warm spices, the earthy pumpkin, the perfect sweetness—but spooned it into glasses instead of a crust. After adding a dollop of whipped cream, an instant classic was born.

1 ¾ cups half-and-half

1 ¾ cups whole milk

3 egg yolks

3 tablespoons cornstarch

One 15-ounce can unsweet-
   ened solid-pack pumpkin

1 cup dark brown sugar

1 teaspoon salt

⅛ teaspoon ground nutmeg

⅛ teaspoon ground ginger

½ teaspoon ground
   cinnamon

1 teaspoon vanilla extract

1. In a medium saucepan vigorously whisk together all of the ingredients except for the vanilla.

2. Cook over medium heat, whisking constantly, until thickened, 10 minutes. (Once you can lift the whisk from the pudding and it leaves a faint shadow, it's done.)

3. Strain the pudding through a fine-mesh sieve into a bowl, pressing pudding through sieve with a ladle (using a ladle here really helps separate the pumpkin solids from the silky pudding). Whisk in vanilla.

4. Cool at room temperature for 10 minutes, press a layer of plastic wrap onto the surface of the pudding, and chill completely in refrigerator, 2 hours.

SUGGESTED PAIRING: Graham Crumbs (page 56) and Whipped Cream (page 66)

EGGNOG PUDDING · {SERVES 4-6}

Just the littlest sip of eggnog can make you feel so good around the holidays—or any time of the year, for that matter! It's like drinking a cup of spiced, melted vanilla ice cream, and in my book that's heaven. Sweetened condensed milk is the only sweetener in this recipe, and its slight caramel notes lend depth and complexity to the pudding. If you close your eyes and have a spoonful, you may just begin to hear sleigh bells ringing.

2 cups whole milk

One 14-ounce can sweetened condensed milk

3 tablespoons cornstarch

3 egg yolks

Scant 1/2 teaspoon nutmeg

1/8 teaspoon salt

1 tablespoon dark rum

1 teaspoon vanilla extract

1. In a medium saucepan whisk together milk, sweetened condensed milk, cornstarch, egg yolks, nutmeg, and salt.

2. Cook over medium heat, whisking constantly, until pudding begins to thicken, 8–9 minutes. (Once you can lift the whisk from the pudding and it leaves a faint shadow, it's done. Pudding will seem fairly loose, but it will thicken up further as it chills.)

3. Strain the pudding through a fine-mesh sieve into a bowl, pressing pudding through sieve with a spatula. Whisk in rum and vanilla.

4. Cool at room temperature for 10 minutes, press a layer of plastic wrap onto the surface of the pudding, and chill completely in refrigerator, 2 hours.

SUGGESTED PAIRING: Cranberry, Orange, and Ginger Compote (page 64)

CHAPTER

TOPPINGS

IF PUDDINGS ARE THE BASIS FOR A DESSERT WARDROBE, THEN THESE RECIPES are the perfect accessories. Making everything from scratch at Puddin' sometimes seems like a lot of work, but just how worthwhile it is becomes perfectly clear when we top a cup of pudding with any of these accompaniments. Not only do they add a unique flavor and texture all their own, but they enhance every pudding they're served with. Feel free to be creative, mixing and matching toppings to suit your every whim.

LIME ANGEL FOOD
CAKE CRUMBS · { MAKES 6 CUPS CRUMBS }

I love this citrusy topping, adapted from Cook's Illustrated's The Best Recipe, not only because it soaks up the flavor of its accompanying pudding while imparting a great cakey texture, but also because it's nearly fat free. As delicious by the slice as it is nestled between layers of pudding, this cake is also an excellent way to use your leftover egg whites.

1 ½ cups sugar, divided

1 cup cake flour

12 egg whites

1 teaspoon cream of tartar

¼ teaspoon salt

1 ½ teaspoons lime juice

Finely grated zest of one lime

1 tablespoon coconut milk

1. Preheat oven to 350°F. Coat the bottom and sides of an angel food cake pan with cooking spray, then line with parchment paper.

2. In a small bowl whisk ¾ cup sugar and flour and set aside.

3. In the bowl of a stand mixer fitted with the whisk attachment, beat whites until frothy, then add cream of tartar and salt and beat on medium-high speed until light and fluffy, 4–5 minutes.

4. Add the remaining ¾ cup sugar to the egg whites, 1 tablespoon at a time, and whip until shiny and soft peaks form, 1–2 minutes. Add lime juice and zest, whip an additional 30 seconds, then add coconut milk and whip an additional 30 seconds.

5. Lower speed, fold in reserved flour-sugar mixture, and beat on medium speed until fully incorporated, 1 additional minute.

6. Transfer the batter to the prepared pan and bake until browned on top, 38–40 minutes.

7. Remove from oven and cool in pan 10 minutes, then turn out onto a cooling rack and cool completely, 30 minutes more.

8. Crumble cake and serve layered with pudding of your choice.

BROWNIE CRUMBS

By now you know that I'm more of a vanilla kind of girl, but I could eat these brownies, adapted from *The Barefoot Contessa Cookbook*, over and over again. The deep chocolate flavor, the smoky coffee edge—what more can I say? These are meant to be crumbled up as a topping for your puddings, but the recipe makes enough for you to keep some of them whole for snacking.

1½ **sticks butter, melted**

12 **ounces bittersweet chocolate (70% cocoa), finely chopped, divided**

1 **ounce unsweetened chocolate, finely chopped**

3/4 **cup sugar**

2 **eggs**

4 **teaspoons instant espresso powder**

1 **tablespoon vanilla extract**

1 3/4 **cups all-purpose flour**

2 **teaspoons baking soda**

1 **teaspoon kosher salt**

1. Preheat oven to 350°F. Spray a 9-by-9-inch pan with cooking spray.

2. In a double boiler combine the butter, 6 ounces of the bittersweet chocolate, and the unsweetened chocolate and cook, stirring, until melted, 5–6 minutes. Remove bowl from heat and cool 30 minutes.

3. In a separate bowl whisk together the sugar, eggs, espresso powder, and vanilla.

4. Add egg mixture to chocolate mixture and whisk until fully incorporated.

5. In a third bowl toss the remaining bittersweet chocolate with the flour, baking soda, and salt. Using a spatula, fold into the chocolate mixture.

6. Pour batter into the prepared pan and bake until a toothpick comes out clean, 30–35 minutes.

7. Cool to room temperature, crumble, and serve layered with pudding of your choice.

CHOCOWICH BITS · { MAKES 12 SANDWICH COOKIES OR 3 CUPS COOKIE CRUMBS }

I've always been obsessed with that famous chocolate sandwich cookie, but not for the reasons you might think. It's not the dark chocolate or even the filling, but rather the hauntingly subtle hint of salt that lingers after you take a bite. After much trial and error, I think I've succeeded in approximating the effect. In my version, kosher salt adds a familiar taste that you won't quite be able to place.

FOR COOKIES:

- 10 tablespoons butter, softened
- ½ cup sugar
- ¼ cup light brown sugar
- 1 egg
- ½ teaspoon vanilla extract
- 1 cup plus 3 tablespoons all-purpose flour
- 1 cup cocoa powder
- 2 tablespoons kosher salt

FOR FILLING:

- 1 stick butter, softened
- 1 cup vegetable shortening, room temperature
- 2 cups confectioners' sugar
- 2 teaspoons vanilla extract

MAKE COOKIES:

1. In a standard mixer fitted with the paddle attachment, beat the butter, sugar, and brown sugar until fluffy, 1–2 minutes.

2. Add egg and vanilla and continue to mix, stopping and scraping down sides of mixer if necessary, an additional 1–2 minutes.

3. In a separate bowl whisk together flour and cocoa powder.

4. With mixer in off position, add flour-cocoa mixture to bowl, then turn mixer

back on at low speed and mix until incorporated, scraping down sides of bowl if necessary, about 1–2 minutes.

5. Turn dough out onto a clean work surface, flatten into a 4-inch-diameter disk, wrap in plastic wrap, and chill in refrigerator until solid, 2 hours. Remove dough from refrigerator 30 minutes before using, to soften slightly.

6. Preheat oven to 350°F.

7. Sprinkle 2 parchment-lined cookie sheets with the salt and set aside.

8. On a clean, lightly floured work surface roll out cookie dough ¼ inch thick.

9. Using a 4-inch round cookie cutter, cut out as many cookies as you can (you should end up with 24 cookies total). Using an offset spatula, transfer the cookies to the salted cookie sheet. You can lay these cookies practically right next to each other since they won't spread out much while baking. Gather remaining dough scraps into a ball, chilling slightly in refrigerator if necessary, and reroll to form more cookies. Roll away—this dough can take it!

10. Bake the cookies until they smell like deeply toasted cocoa, 15–20 minutes.

11. Remove the cookies from the oven and cool completely on the cookie sheet.

MAKE FILLING:

1. In the bowl of a stand mixer fitted with the paddle attachment, beat butter and shortening until smooth.

2. With mixer in off position, add confectioners' sugar to bowl. Beat on medium-low speed until incorporated, scraping down sides of bowl if necessary.

3. Add vanilla, then beat on high speed until super-creamy and fluffy, 3–4 minutes.

ASSEMBLE COOKIES:

1. Transfer filling to a pastry bag or a ziplock bag with one bottom corner snipped off.

CONTINUED

2. Arrange half the cookies salt-side down and pipe 2 tablespoons filling per cookie, leaving a ½-inch border around the edges.

3. Top each with a second cookie, salt-side up, gently pressing down so the filling spreads to the edges of the cookies.

4. Chill cookies for 30 minutes. Eat as is or crumble into bits and layer with your choice of pudding.

GINGER CRUNCH

There may be months when I obsess over this pudding or that topping, but these buttery squares are consistently fetish-worthy in my book. It all started when my mom was hired to make desserts for a New Zealand–owned bakery and she was gifted this recipe by talented antipodean pastry chef Sue Boyer. Everyone went bonkers for the crunchy cookie base, spicy flavor, and lush, velvety texture. Finely crushed, they add the perfect buttery zing to citrus puddings. You can also store them whole in the fridge or freezer, then serve them cold—the chewy texture and sneaky heat will have you coming back for more!

2½ sticks butter, softened, divided

¾ cup sugar

2¼ cups all-purpose flour

1½ teaspoons baking powder

1 cup confectioners' sugar

3 tablespoons Lyle's Golden Syrup or light corn syrup

3½ tablespoons powdered ginger

1. Preheat oven to 350°F. Coat a 10-by-12-inch rimmed baking sheet with cooking spray, top with a piece of parchment paper, spray again, and set aside.

2. In a standard mixer fitted with the paddle attachment, beat 1¼ sticks of the butter and the sugar until fluffy, 3 minutes. Mixture will appear dry; the longer you beat it, the better.

3. With the mixer in the off position, add the flour and baking powder. Beat on low speed to blend, then increase speed to medium and mix until fully incorporated, scraping down sides of bowl once, 1–2 minutes.

4. Dump the dough onto the prepared baking sheet. Initially it won't look like enough dough, but trust me, it is. Press dough into pan as evenly as you can, making sure it's as flat as possible. Use the bottom of a measuring cup or a glass to help press down the dough if you'd like.

CONTINUED

5. Bake until the center of the dough is pale and the edges are just starting to brown, 20 minutes. (Dough may puff during baking; this is okay!)

6. While dough is baking, in a medium saucepan combine remaining 1¼ sticks butter, the confectioners' sugar, golden syrup, and ginger. Bring to boil, then reduce heat and simmer until syrup thickens and begins to pull away from sides of saucepan, 2 minutes.

7. Remove baking sheet from oven and immediately pour syrup over the cookie slab. Cut the slab into 20 two-inch squares.

8. Cool completely and eat as is or crumble on your pudding of choice.

GRAHAM CRACKERS • { MAKES 24 GRAHAM CRACKERS }

Not really a cracker, and somehow not quite cookie material, either, graham crackers are a dessert with a bit of an identity crisis. They started out as a health-food item containing a special type of flour, but these days most don't contain actual graham flour. For authenticity's sake I like to use the original item—the real deal should contain visible darker brown flecks of wheat bran and germ. I toast the graham flour to give it extra depth, then blend it with two other varieties for a perfect trio that combines tenderness and crispiness in every bite. Adding a touch of black pepper gives the cookies a slightly spicy edge.

½ cup graham flour
  (preferably Bob's Red Mill)

1 cup whole-wheat flour

¾ cup all-purpose flour

1 teaspoon salt

½ teaspoon baking soda

½ teaspoon ground cinnamon

¼ teaspoon freshly ground black
  pepper

2 tablespoons butter,
  softened

2 tablespoons vegetable
  shortening,
  room temperature

⅓ cup light brown sugar

2 eggs

¼ cup honey

2 teaspoons vanilla extract

1. Preheat oven to 350°F.

2. Spread graham flour evenly on a parchment-lined rimmed baking sheet. Bake, stirring after 10 minutes, until flour darkens in color (but isn't *too* dark) and smells roasty-toasty, 20 minutes total. Cool completely.

3. In a large bowl, whisk together graham flour, whole-wheat flour, all-purpose flour, salt, baking soda, cinnamon, and pepper and set aside.

4. In the bowl of a stand mixer fitted with the paddle attachment, beat together the butter, shortening, brown sugar, and eggs on medium-high speed until incorporated, 30 seconds.

CONTINUED

5. Add honey and vanilla and beat until smooth, an additional 1 minute.

6. With the mixer running at low speed, add half the dry ingredients to the mixer and beat until just incorporated, 1 minute. Stop mixer, scape down sides of bowl, add the remaining dry ingredients, return to medium-high speed, and mix until just incorporated, an additional 30–60 seconds, being careful not to overmix. (The dough will be very soft.) Collect dough, wrap in plastic wrap, and chill in refrigerator at least 4 hours or overnight and dream about how good these graham crackers are going to be.

7. On a piece of parchment paper, roll out dough into a ¼-inch-thick rectangle, about 10 x 15 inches.

8. Using a pizza cutter, or a knife and ruler, score dough into twenty-four 2½-inch squares. Using a fork or pastry docker, prick holes in each cookie in whatever pattern you desire.

9. Separate dough rectangles and transfer to a parchment-lined cookie sheet, arranging ½ inch apart (cookies will hardly spread).

10. Bake until golden brown, 17–18 minutes. Cool at room temperature before serving.

. . . .

GRAHAM CRUMBS · MAKES 2 CUPS CRUMBS

11 Graham Crackers (page 55) or five 2 ½-by-5-inch sheets of store-bought graham crackers

1 stick butter, melted

¼ cup light brown sugar

1. Preheat oven to 350°F.

2. Place graham crackers in a food processor and process until fine crumbs form, 30 seconds.

3. Transfer crumbs to a bowl, add melted butter and brown sugar, and stir until crumbs are moistened.

4. Spread crumbs evenly on a parchment-lined rimmed baking sheet and bake, stirring every 5 minutes, until toasted and fragrant, 12-14 minutes.

5. Remove from oven and cool completely at room temperature. Layer with your pudding of choice.

VANILLA WAFERS

Getting the right combination of tenderness and crispy edges took some time, but now that I have it down I can hardly make these little round beauties fast enough. They're a great topper for any of our puddings, but I dare you to get that far without sneaking one by itself, dunked into a glass of milk.

3/4 cup sugar

1/4 cup confectioners' sugar

1 stick butter, softened

1/2 teaspoon salt

2 eggs

1 tablespoon whole milk

1 teaspoon vanilla extract

1½ cups all-purpose flour

1 teaspoon baking powder

1. Preheat oven to 350°F.

2. In the bowl of a stand mixer fitted with the paddle attachment, cream sugar, confectioners' sugar, butter, and salt on high speed until light and fluffy, 3–4 minutes total, scraping down sides of bowl if necessary.

3. Lower speed to medium and add eggs one at a time, beating after each addition until incorporated.

4. Add the milk and vanilla and beat until incorporated, 1 minute.

5. Turn mixer off, add flour and baking powder, return speed to medium, and beat until it looks like a thick spread, 2–3 minutes. Chill dough in refrigerator for at least 30 minutes.

6. Drop batter by heaping teaspoonfuls about 1 inch apart onto 2 parchment-lined cookie sheets (the batter dots may look small, but they spread out quite a bit when baking).

7. Bake, rotating cookie sheets after 7 minutes, until browned around the edges and pale in the middle, 15 minutes. Cool completely on cookie sheet.

SALTED CARAMEL SAUCE · { MAKES 2 CUPS }

I've been told I can be a little dramatic, but sometimes a little excitement is perfectly justified, don't you think? Here is my ode to Salted Caramel Sauce: *I would bathe in thee if I could, and on more than one occasion I've been tempted to drink thee from a giant trough with a golden straw.* The secret to great caramel sauce? Don't stir! Sugar and water are like a happily married couple, and the spoon is the mistress; once the spoon gets involved, the marriage sours. The moral of the story? Leave that water and sugar alone, and you and this luscious sauce will have a great long-term relationship, too.

1 cup sugar

2 tablespoons corn syrup

1/8 teaspoon cream of tartar

1 cup heavy cream

1 tablespoon butter

1/2 teaspoon vanilla extract

1 teaspoon sea salt
(or more to taste)

1. In a medium saucepan combine sugar, 1/2 cup water, corn syrup, and cream of tartar. Bring to a boil over medium-high heat, stirring only once or twice to help sugar dissolve.

2. Once the sugar is dissolved, boil the mixture, without stirring, until it turns a golden amber hue along the sides, 7–8 minutes.

3. Using an oven mitt, grab the handle and swirl the pot; this will help blend the cooked and uncooked portions. (This process reminds me of mixing paint.)

4. Once all of the sugar is a dark rich golden color, add the cream, butter, vanilla, and salt and stir; mixture will bubble and steam before everything comes together. Turn off heat and allow sauce to sit in the pot for 1–2 minutes before pouring into a bowl to cool to room temperature.

FUDGE SAUCE · {MAKES 1½ CUPS}

This thick fudge sauce gets an extra layer of delish from the addition of crème fraîche, which is basically cream that's been left to sour a bit. You may have to pay attention to know it's there, but that slight hint of tanginess transforms a simple chocolate confection into something otherworldly.

⅔ cup heavy cream

½ cup light corn syrup

⅓ cup crème fraîche

⅓ cup dark brown sugar

¼ cup cocoa powder

¼ teaspoon salt

6 ounces bittersweet chocolate (70% cocoa), chopped

2 tablespoons butter

1 teaspoon vanilla extract

1. Combine heavy cream, corn syrup, crème fraîche, brown sugar, cocoa, salt, and chocolate in a small saucepan.

2. Bring to a low boil, reduce heat, and simmer, whisking vigorously until thickened, 5 minutes.

3. Remove from heat and whisk in butter and vanilla.

4. Transfer to a bowl. Serve right away, like hot fudge, or cool to room temperature and serve, thick and rich, with pudding.

Vegan Fudge Sauce

FOR A RICH AND CREAMY VEGAN VARIATION, omit the butter and replace the heavy cream and crème fraîche with 1 cup of coconut milk.

DULCE DE LECHE · {MAKES 1½ CUPS}

I originally created this recipe for use in my Dulce de Leche Pudding (page 27), but it was too good to sideline merely as an ingredient in one recipe. So here it is in all its golden glory, ready to be spooned onto the pudding of your choice (or turned into national currency). Making dulce de leche right in the can is an age-old tradition in Latin countries; the technique is simple, the finished product irresistible. Opening the can after cooking is a revelation, as the condensed milk has become super-thick and dark—the most gorgeous golden hue you've ever seen in your entire life.

One 14-ounce can sweetened condensed milk

1. Place an unopened 14-ounce can of sweetened condensed milk in a small saucepan. Fill the saucepan with water until it comes ¾ of the way up the sides of the can.

2. Bring the saucepan to a boil over high heat, then turn down to a strong simmer. Let simmer at least 3 hours and up to 5 hours, flipping the can every 30 minutes and adding more water whenever the level drops to the halfway point on the sides of the can.

3. Using a jar lifter, tongs, or heatproof oven mitt, remove can from water and let cool at room temperature until easy to handle, 30 minutes. Serve warm or at room temperature.

BLACKBERRY COMPOTE · {MAKES 1½ CUPS}

In this compote the combination of berries and wine creates an almost Port-like syrup, and the surprise of lime gives a zingy edge that makes this great as a topper for Hevra's Lemon Obsession Pudding, Happens-to-Be-Vegan Coconut Pudding, or Key Lime Pudding.

1½ cups fresh blackberries, divided

¼ cup dry, fruity red wine

¼ cup sugar

2 tablespoons lime juice

In a small saucepan combine ¾ cup blackberries, wine, sugar, and lime juice. Bring to a boil, remove from heat, stir in remaining blackberries, and cool to room temperature.

. . . .

CHERRY COMPOTE · {MAKES 2½ CUPS}

For this tart-sweet compote, make sure to use Montmorency cherries, a delicious sour variety that imparts a puckery sweetness to the finished product. Though I love this compote best on Vanilla Pudding, it's also great on your morning oatmeal, spooned onto angel food cake, or on top of a bowl of Greek yogurt.

1½ cups dry, fruity red wine

½ cup sugar

2 cups pitted dried sweetened cherries

1. Combine wine, ¾ cup water, and sugar in a small saucepan and bring to a boil.

2. Remove from heat, add cherries, let sit in hot liquid for 5 minutes. Compote may be served warm or cold, and can be stored in the refrigerator in an airtight container or ziplock bag for up to a week.

CRANBERRY, ORANGE, AND GINGER COMPOTE

• { MAKES 2 CUPS }

I developed this specifically to go with my Christmas Parfait (page 82), but it would be equally good stirred into a bowl of Greek yogurt or even used as a condiment for a holiday dinner. The addition of fresh ginger really sets this compote apart from others I've tasted.

One 12-ounce bag fresh cranberries

3/4 cup sugar

1/2 cup orange juice

Zest of 1/2 orange

1 tablespoon finely grated ginger

Combine cranberries, 3/4 cup water, sugar, orange juice, and zest in a medium saucepan and bring to a boil. Reduce heat and simmer until cranberries break up and mixture thickens, 15–20 minutes. Stir in ginger during last minute of cooking. Cool. Compote can be stored in the refrigerator in an airtight container or ziplock bag for up to a week.

· ·

PEACH MELBA TOPPING • { MAKES 3 CUPS }

I first discovered Peach Melba in high school, during a somewhat misguided phase of attempting low-fat recipes. (What was I thinking?) Created by the renowned chef Auguste Escoffier in honor of Australian opera singer Nellie Melba, this mixture of fresh fruit and sugar, cooked simply, is light and indulgent at the same time.

1/4 cup sugar

3 ripe peaches, peeled, pitted, and chopped (3 cups) or two 10-ounce packages of frozen sliced peaches, thawed

3/4 cup raspberries

In a medium saucepan bring sugar and 1/4 cup water to a boil. Add peaches and simmer until slightly softened, 3 minutes. Remove from heat and add berries. Cool to room temperature, then chill in refrigerator. Compote can be stored in the refrigerator in an airtight container or ziplock bag for up to a week.

MAPLE-APPLE TOPPING · {MAKES 2 CUPS}

Great as part of our Breakfast of Champions Parfait (page 75), this light, maple-laced topping is best when made with Grade B maple syrup, which is typically darker and more liquidy than Grade A syrup and imbued with notes of smoke and wood—almost like a fine bourbon.

1/4 cup butter

2 large, crisp apples (about 1 lb total), peeled, cored, and cut into small dice

3/4 teaspoon cinnamon

1/2 cup maple syrup

1/4 teaspoon salt

1. Heat butter in a small saucepan over medium heat until golden and flecked with tiny toasty bits, 1–2 minutes.

2. Add apples and cinnamon and cook until apples are slightly softened, 5 minutes.

3. Add maple syrup and salt, bring to a boil, then reduce heat and simmer an additional 2 minutes. Remove from heat and cool to room temperature. Serve warm or at room temperature. Topping can be stored in the refrigerator in an airtight container or ziplock bag for up to a week

WHIPPED CREAM · {MAKES 2 CUPS}

Unsweetened whipped cream is the perfect foil for pudding's richness. The pureness of the unadorned cream, whipped into a pillowy cloud, cuts the sweetness of the pudding and imparts a simple, airy elegance.

1 cup chilled heavy cream

In the bowl of a stand mixer fitted with the whisk attachment, whip cream on high speed until soft peaks form, 1–2 minutes.

. . . .

CARAMEL WHIPPED CREAM · {MAKES 2¼ CUPS}

Take whipped cream. Add caramel sauce. Whip some more. Enjoy—I mean, become obsessed. Really, really obsessed, as we do at the shop. I'd spackle the walls with this stuff if I could! The caramel adds additional body to the cream without diminishing its volume, essentially creating golden clouds. Trust me—you'll want to float away with a bowlful.

1 cup chilled heavy cream

⅔ cup Salted Caramel Sauce (page 58), chilled

1. In the bowl of a stand mixer fitted with the whisk attachment, whip cream on high speed until soft peaks form, 1–2 minutes.

2. Add Salted Caramel Sauce and whip until soft peaks return, an additional 2 minutes.

MARSHMALLOW CRÈME · {MAKES 5 CUPS}

When I think of my favorite dessert memories from childhood, Marshmallow Fluff is a part of many of them. We always had some on hand, which eased my anxiety about a shortage, but the downside was that I was often busted with spoon in hand, digging directly into the tub. Making my own, I based the recipe on a classic French meringue. Make sure the bowl of your mixer is spotlessly clean and free of any oil, which can inhibit the egg whites from fluffing up into the giant puffs of goodness they are destined to become. At Puddin', I'll lavish a cup of pudding with Marshmallow Crème, then quickly brown the top with my handy kitchen torch; feel free to do the same at home.

2 egg whites

1 cup corn syrup

¼ teaspoon salt

1 cup confectioners' sugar

1½ teaspoons vanilla extract

1. In the bowl of a stand mixer fitted with the whisk attachment, beat egg whites, corn syrup, and salt on high speed until big and fluffy, like a giant candy cloud, 4–5 minutes.

2. Turn off mixer and add confectioners' sugar and vanilla. Turn mixer back on low and beat until sugar is incorporated, then raise speed to high and whip until the contents of the bowl look like a mass of shiny white plastic, 3 additional minutes.

CANDIED MIXED NUTS · {MAKES 3 CUPS}

Creamy things and crunchy things are a natural pair, which is why these mixed nuts work so well with our puddings. I've suggested a particular mix of nuts here, but feel free to swap in your favorites according to your whim. I love using Lyle's Golden Syrup, a British import that's a lot more interesting than honey or corn syrup. For starters, it has a mellow flavor that falls somewhere between maple syrup and butterscotch. Then there's the decorative tin or jar, which you can wash out, dry, and reuse to store these nuts or anything else that comes to mind.

1 cup unsalted pecans

3/4 cup unsalted almonds

1/2 cup raw unsalted peanuts

1/2 cup raw walnuts

6 tablespoons Lyle's Golden Syrup or light corn syrup

1/3 cup sugar

1 teaspoon salt

1. Preheat oven to 350°F.

2. In a large bowl combine pecans, almonds, peanuts, and walnuts. Stir in syrup, sugar, and salt until nuts are coated evenly

3. Spread nuts evenly on a parchment-lined rimmed baking sheet. Bake, stirring after 10 minutes, until nuts darken and smell toasted and fragrant, 20 minutes.

4. Remove from oven and cool completely, 30 minutes. Break up nuts and serve on top of your pudding of choice. Nuts can be stored in an airtight container for up to 3 weeks.

PEANUT BRITTLE BITS · {MAKES 3 CUPS}

There's always that moment when you take a bite of a great piece of peanut brittle and realize that there's something else going on. Sure, it's crunchy, but there's also a tiny bit of airiness, which prevents the candy from shattering a tooth with every bite. As I learned at the Culinary Institute of America, the secret is baking soda, which aerates the caramel and creates a slightly forgiving texture. That, combined with the softer crunch of whole peanuts, makes for one of the store's most popular toppings.

3/4 cup plus 2 tablespoons sugar

3/4 cup corn syrup

1 cup salted peanuts

1 tablespoon butter

1 teaspoon vanilla extract

1/2 teaspoon baking soda

1. In a medium saucepan, combine sugar, corn syrup, and 1/4 cup plus 2 tablespoons water. Bring to a boil over medium heat, stirring only once or twice.

2. Continue to boil without stirring, until liquid turns golden around the edges, 10–12 minutes, then grab the handle and swirl the pan.

3. Add the peanuts and continue to cook, swirling the pan until the mixture is a lovely golden amber hue.

4. Remove from heat, add the butter, vanilla, and baking soda, and stir.

5. Pour the mixture onto a parchment-lined rimmed baking sheet. Cool at room temperature until the mixture forms one giant slab and is hard to the touch.

7. Break the slab up with a rolling pin to form gorgeous pieces of brittle bark or, for more finely crumbled bits, place pieces of brittle in a ziplock bag and crush with a rolling pin. Serve alongside or layered with your pudding of choice. Peanut brittle can be stored in an airtight container for up to 3 weeks.

SPRINKLES · { MAKES 1 CUP }

Few things give me more pleasure than taking an item that's usually mass-produced in a nameless factory and developing a recipe for it. I've always adored the way sprinkles linger on the tongue, and opening the shop gave me the opportunity to develop my own recipe for these delightful confections. Of all the house-made items we produce at Puddin', these colorful bits of candy generate some of the highest levels of excitement. The recipe is a basic royal icing, colored however you like, and piped from a pastry bag fitted with the teeniest piping tip known to mankind. Make a double batch, throw the extras in some cellophane bags, and give these confetti-like bits as gifts.

1 egg white

¼ teaspoon vanilla extract

Pinch salt

2 cups confectioners' sugar

1–2 drops food coloring (see note)

1. In a small bowl combine egg white, vanilla, and salt. Add confectioners' sugar until a super-thick white paste forms. Add food coloring and stir until evenly incorporated.

2. Fit a pastry bag with a #2 pastry tip and transfer mixture to pastry bag.

3. On a parchment-lined rimmed baking sheet pipe the mixture into one long, continuous string, moving from one end of the sheet to the other as though you were arranging a long piece of yarn on the sheet. You'll need extra muscle power to pipe these, but it's worth it! Don't worry if the string breaks at points.

4. Allow the sprinkles to dry, uncovered, at room temperature in a dry environment, for at least 12 hours and up to 24.

5. Run a pastry scraper up and down across the rows of dried sprinkle strings; they'll naturally break up, but you can break them further with your hands if you want. Sprinkles can be stored in an airtight container for up to three weeks.

NOTE: For rainbow sprinkles, double the recipe and divide the mixture among 4–6 bowls before adding the food coloring. Once divided, color each bowl to your liking and proceed with Step 2 of the recipe.

PUDDING PARFAITS

PARFAITS ARE AN OBVIOUS USE FOR PUDDING, ALLOWING YOU TO MIX and match the silky layers to your heart's content. Perhaps because they're so customizable, parfaits have proven to be a big success at the shop. We sell them premade in tall, clear cups, so that everyone can see their striated glory. The possible combinations for parfaits are truly endless. Here I've included our greatest hits, but remember, these are just suggestions. Feel free to swap in different toppings, puddings, and compotes to fulfill your own parfait predilections.

BALD MAN'S BANANA CREAM DREAM PARFAIT

{ SERVES 5 }

I've named this parfait after a smooth-headed customer who always brings a lady friend into the shop with him and orders this parfait—but never shares with her. This one's all for you, honey! I love the way the crunchy crumbs at the bottom make you dig down deep into the cup.

3/4 cup Graham Crumbs
  (page 56)

1 recipe Banana Pudding
  (page 8), divided

3/4 cup Banana Upside-Down
  Cake layers, crumbled
  (page 91)

1/3 cup Whipped Cream
  (page 66)

Layer graham crumbs, half of the pudding, cake crumbs, whipped cream, and remaining pudding in 5 serving glasses.

BREAKFAST OF CHAMPIONS PARFAIT · { SERVES 4 }

When you spend as much time as we do at Puddin', you find yourself eating meals at odd hours. Once, when we were craving breakfast, I ran out, gathered all the ingredients for a classic breakfast, and next thing we knew, this amazing parfait materialized.

1 recipe Maple Pudding (page 41),
  divided

6 tablespoons chopped leftover
  pancakes of your choice.

4 tablespoons Maple-Apple
  Topping (page 65)

4 tablespoons extra-crisp cooked
  crumbled bacon

Layer half of the pudding, chopped pancakes, maple-apple topping, and remaining pudding in 4 serving glasses. Garnish with crumbled bacon.

Bald Man's Banana Cream Dream Parfait

CARAMEL MACCHIATO PARFAIT

{ SERVES 10 }

When I first opened Puddin' I was so busy I couldn't even get to the coffee shop for my favorite coffee drink. This parfait (accompanied by many cups of plain coffee) was an able substitute.

½ cup Fudge Sauce (page 61)

1 recipe Chocolate Pudding (page 3)

1 cup Brownie Crumbs (page 49)

1 cup Salted Caramel Sauce (page 58)

1 recipe Coffee Pudding (page 10)

Layer fudge sauce, chocolate pudding, brownie crumbs, caramel sauce, and coffee pudding in 8 serving glasses.

- -

CLASSIC PARFAIT · { SERVES 10 }

Talk about sentimental value: this was the first pudding cup I ever made for the shop. It was inspired by the Jell-O pudding cups that fueled my childhood in Ohio.

1 recipe Chocolate Pudding (page 3)

1¼ cups Whipped Cream (page 66)

1 recipe Butterscotch Pudding (page 5)

Divide chocolate pudding evenly among 10 serving glasses. Layer with whipped cream and top with butterscotch pudding.

Caramel Macchiato Parfait

BIRTHDAY CAKE PARFAIT · {SERVES 5}

Who doesn't like celebrating a birthday? With this parfait, you can party like you were born on this very day. Naturally, I recommend an all-vanilla parfait because that's what I'd want for my birthday, but feel free to customize!

1¼ cups cake crumbs
(see note page 112), divided

1 cup Sprinkles (page 70),
divided

1 recipe Vanilla Pudding
(page 4), divided

Layer ½ of the cake crumbs, ⅓ of the sprinkles, and ½ of the pudding in 5 serving glasses. Repeat. Garnish with remaining sprinkles.

. . . .

S'MORES PARFAIT · {SERVES 8}

It's my belief that everyone should own a kitchen torch. Aside from adding the signature glassy top to crème brûlée, this fairly inexpensive kitchen gadget can be used to create a pleasing toasted topping wherever your little pudding-loving heart desires. In this case, I believe you'll desire that topping for my Marshmallow Crème. The gorgeous golden-brown top will take you straight back to the campfire.

1½ cups Graham Crumbs
(page 56), divided

1 recipe Chocolate Pudding
(page 3)

2 cups Marshmallow Crème
(page 67)

Layer half of the graham crumbs, the chocolate pudding, remaining graham crumbs, and marshmallow crème in 8 serving dishes. Using a kitchen torch, brown the top of the Marshmallow Crème until lightly browned.

Birthday Cake Parfait

LEMON DROP PARFAIT · {SERVES 5}

I am so taken with Ginger Crunch, I had to find a way to use it in as many novel ways as possible. Lemon and ginger take to each other like long-lost friends, so this is a natural combination.

1 recipe Hevra's Lemon
  Obsession Pudding
  (page 11), divided

²⁄₃ cup Ginger Crunch
  (page 53)

1²⁄₃ cup Marshmallow Crème
  (page 67)

Layer half of the pudding, Ginger Crunch, and remaining pudding in 5 serving glasses. Top with marshmallow crème. Brown the top of each parfait with a kitchen torch if desired.

· ·

COCONUT CRUISE PARFAIT · {SERVES 4}

A taste of the tropics right on this very page!

½ cup Graham Crumbs
  (page 56)

1 recipe Happens-to-be-
  Vegan Coconut Pudding
  (page 18), divided

¼ cup Lime Angel Food
  Cake Crumbs (page 48)

¼ cup chopped fresh
  pineapple

Layer graham crumbs, half of the pudding, angel food cake crumbs, pineapple, and remaining pudding in 4 serving dishes.

Lemon Drop Parfait

CHRISTMAS PARFAIT · {SERVES 4}

Eggnog, ginger-tinged cranberries, graham crackers—it must be the holidays! Assemble this dessert to cap off a festive meal, and you may leave panettone, linzer tortes, and hot cross buns behind forever.

1 recipe Eggnog Pudding
(page 44), divided

½ cup Graham Crumbs
(page 56)

½ cup Cranberry, Orange,
and Ginger Compote
(page 64)

Layer half of the pudding, graham crumbs, compote, and remaining pudding in 4 serving glasses.

· ·

DA DECADENT PARFAIT · {SERVES 6}

My Peanut Butter Pudding is one of my richest creations, and I had a couple of customers who regularly ordered a whole cupful but could only finish half. I thought I'd "lighten" it by serving it with fudge sauce, when in fact that only made it more indulgent. I named this parfait "Da Decadent" to mentally prepare those brave souls who make it for what's coming!

1 cup Fudge Sauce (page 61),
divided

1 recipe Peanut Butter Pudding
(page 25), divided

3/4 cup Brownie Crumbs
(page 49)

1½ cups Whipped Cream
(page 66)

Layer half of the fudge sauce, half of the pudding, remaining fudge sauce, brownie crumbs, and remaining pudding in 6 serving dishes. Top with whipped cream.

Christmas Parfait

PEACH MELBA PARFAIT · {SERVES 6}

Come summer, few things please me as much as a ripe, juicy peach. I created this parfait to conjure up that enjoyment by layering Peach Melba Topping and my signature Vanilla Pudding with a drizzle of complex balsamic vinegar and a scattering of crunchy ginger-flavored cookies. It reminds me of those simple, delicious desserts you get in Italy in the summer—minus the plane ticket.

⅓ cup Ginger Crunch
  (page 53)

1 recipe Vanilla Pudding
  (page 4), divided

¾ cup Peach Melba Topping
  (page 64)

1 tablespoon good-quality
  balsamic vinegar

Layer ginger crunch, half of the pudding, and peach melba topping in 6 serving dishes. Drizzle with balsamic vinegar and top with remaining pudding.

HIERONYMUS BOSCH PARFAIT · {SERVES 6-8}

Growing up, I had quite a collection of children's books, and Pish, Posh, Said Hieronymus Bosch, the story of the famous Dutch artist's housekeeper and the way she dealt with the artist's knickknacks, was one of my favorites. This is the "kitchen sink" parfait to end all others, allowing for combinations that can be taken as far as the imagination allows.

COMBINE TO YOUR LIKING:

3 cups of your favorite
  Puddin' pudding

2 cups assorted cake or
  cookie crumbs (see note
  page 112).

Combine pudding and crumbs in large bowl. Eat immediately or, for an altogether different and amazing creation, cover and chill in refrigerator for up to 24 hours, allowing the crumbs to absorb moisture from the pudding.

Peach Melba Parfait

PUDDING CAKES AND PIES

THERE COULDN'T BE A PUDDIN' SHOP WITHOUT OUR PUDDING CAKES.
When developing the store's menu, I wanted to figure out a way to integrate our puddings into pies and cakes in a way that fully showcased the pudding's creamy goodness. In these recipes, every ingredient has been chosen to best compliment the puddings used, but, as usual, feel free to improvise! And more than in any other chapter, it's essential that you read the whole recipe through from start to finish. Every recipe is built on one of my pudding recipes, so getting the pudding done earlier in the day—or even a day or two in advance—is recommended.

Frosting a Pudding Cake

At first, filling and frosting your pudding cake may seem intimidating, but it's really not that complicated. I've devised a foolproof system to ensure that every cake you frost is pretty and party-ready. A few things to remember when frosting a cake:

. . . .

• START WITH FLAT LAYERS. Depending on the cake pans you use, cake layers can sometimes come out of the oven with a dome-shaped top. If this is the case, make sure to level out your cake layers using a serrated knife; this allows you to create an even surface, so your cake will come out flat on top. Another perk? Leveling leaves you with yummy cake crumbs (see note on page 112), which can be used to top your favorite cup of pudding or in one of our parfaits.

• USE AN OFFSET SPATULA. This baker's staple, whose blade is designed to get closer to the cake's surface than a standard knife can manage, is available in several sizes at kitchen-supply stores. For frosting, a standard 9-inch offset spatula does the trick.

• INVEST IN A LAZY SUSAN. Being able to easily maneuver around a cake while frosting it makes the process infinitely more fun and manageable. A lazy Susan—essentially a rotating plate—does the swiveling work for you, allowing you to rotate the cake with one hand while dealing with the frosting with the other. Rotating cake stands can be found at baking-supply stores, but you can also place a cake pedestal on a standard flat lazy Susan.

• SEAL IN THE PUDDING. Pudding is a fluid entity that needs to be tamed. If left to its own devices, it will flow in any direction like water escaping from a swollen river. That's why it needs to be sealed inside your cake—to prevent what I call "jailbreak pudding." Piping a layer of buttercream frosting near the perimeter of your cake's base layer creates an impenetrable ring into which you can pipe your pudding.

- MASTER THE CRUMB COAT. An unfrosted cake is a thing of beauty, but frosting without a crumb coat—a thin base layer of frosting—can unleash a torrent of tiny cake bits, marring the visual effect of the frosted cake with a sea of tiny speckles. Think of the crumb coat as the primer before the paint. The thin base layer of frosting tricks the cake layers into releasing their bits and keeps them covered up. That way, the final layer of frosting is free to nap the cake without any distractions. The crumb coat should be about an eighth of an inch thick, and don't worry if you have a few naked spots of cake showing through; as long as most of the cake is covered with a thin layer of frosting, you're good to go.

- FROST IT FRESH. My frostings are designed to be used immediately. Fresh out of the mixer, they have a texture that's ideal for spreading and forming lovely, photo shoot–worthy peaks. If you can't use the frosting right away, take it out of the fridge two hours before use, then rewhip at high speed until nice and fluffy.

- REMEMBER THE FINAL FROST. This is your chance to crown the cake for presentation. Centering the final portion of frosting on top of the cake, then working outward, gives you maximum control and helps you easily gauge how much frosting you have left to send down onto the sides of the cake.

- SERVE IT NOW. Cakes are meant to be frosted and eaten right away, but they can safely sit on your countertop under a cake dome for up to a day. At that point, you will need to refrigerate your cake. Cakes will last for 4–5 days in the refrigerator.

BANANA UPSIDE-DOWN CAKE WITH MALTED PUDDING · {SERVES 12}

I'm generally not a fan of extracts, which I consider them to be the flavor equivalent of a person taking a joke just a bit too far. That's why this moist, delicious cake is so darn good—all of its banana flavor comes from the real thing. If you can, make the layers, which I adapted from *The Silver Palate Cookbook,* a day in advance; giving this cake a chance to settle allows it to develop even more flavor. An intriguing middle layer of malted pudding, followed by a halo of walnut-infused frosting, adds up to a cake that feels like a walnut sundae in every slice.

FOR BANANA CAKE:

- ⅔ cup light brown sugar
- 2½ sticks butter, softened, divided
- 3 firm, ripe whole bananas, halved lengthwise, plus 1 cup mashed ripe bananas (you may use mashed bananas reserved from Banana Pudding, page 8)
- ⅔ cup sugar
- 3 eggs, separated
- 2 cups all-purpose flour
- 1 teaspoon baking powder
- ½ teaspoon baking soda
- ½ teaspoon salt
- ½ cup buttermilk, shaken
- 1 teaspoon vanilla extract

FOR BROWN BUTTER WALNUT BUTTERCREAM:

- 1½ sticks plus 3 tablespoons butter
- ⅓ cup walnuts, chopped
- 1 teaspoon kosher salt
- 6 egg whites
- ⅔ cup sugar

FOR ASSEMBLY:

- 1 cup My Bro's Malted Milk Pudding (page 28)
- Simple syrup or melted apricot jam (optional)

CONTINUED

1. Preheat oven to 350°F. Coat two 8-inch round cake layer pans with cooking spray and set aside.

2. In a small saucepan, combine the brown sugar and 1½ sticks butter. Bring to a boil and cook until the sugar is dissolved and the mixture is smooth, 3–4 minutes. Carefully divide the hot mixture evenly between the prepared cake pans. Arrange 3 banana halves cut side down in each of the cake pans and place pans in freezer while making cake batter (this keeps the bananas from shifting when you top them with batter).

3. In the bowl of a stand mixer fitted with the paddle attachment, cream together the remaining 1 stick butter with the sugar at high speed until light and fluffy as a cloud, 4–5 minutes.

4. Add egg yolks one at a time to mixer and beat until mixture is light and fluffy, 1–2 minutes.

5. Add mashed bananas and beat until incorporated, 30 seconds.

6. In a medium bowl whisk together the flour, baking powder, baking soda, and salt. Turn mixer off, add dry ingredients, turn mixer back on to low speed, and slowly increase speed to medium, mixing until dry ingredients are well blended, 1 minute.

7. Add the buttermilk and vanilla extract and mix 1 minute more. Transfer batter to a large bowl and set aside; wash well and thoroughly dry mixing bowl.

8. Fit mixing bowl with whisk attachment, all reserved egg whites, and whisk on high speed until soft peaks form, 1–2 minutes.

9. Using a spatula, stir a small amount of the egg whites into the banana batter to loosen batter slightly. Gently fold the remaining egg whites into the banana batter, being careful not to overstir and deflate the lovely aerated batter.

10. Divide the batter among the prepared cake pans and bake until a cake tester or wooden toothpick inserted into the center comes out clean, 30–35 minutes.

11. Remove from oven and let sit in pan 10 minutes, then turn out onto a cooling rack and cool to room temperature, banana sides up, 30 minutes.

MAKE FROSTING:

1. Preheat oven to 350°F.

2. In a small saucepan, heat 3 tablespoons of butter over medium-high heat until fragrant with brown flecks, 2–3 minutes. Add walnuts and salt to saucepan, toss to coat, and transfer to a parchment-lined rimmed baking sheet.

3. Toast walnuts in oven until fragrant and lightly browned, 5–7 minutes. Let cool at room temperature until easy to handle, then finely process in food processor or finely chop by hand.

4. Set the bowl of a stand mixer atop a saucepan filled with simmering water and whisk egg whites and sugar until warm to the touch.

5. Return bowl with heated mixture to a stand mixer fitted with the whip attachment and whip at high speed until stiff, glossy, and cool, 4–5 minutes.

6. Add remaining butter 1 tablespoon at a time and whip until nice and fluffy, 4–5 minutes.

7. Add chopped nut mixture to bowl and mix until incorporated, 1–2 minutes.

ASSEMBLE CAKE:

1. Place a cake layer on a lazy Susan or large, flat plate, banana side up. (Use the less attractive of the layers for the bottom.) Pipe a ring of buttercream around the top of the cake about ¼ inch from the sides to create a wall. Fill the area inside the ring with the malted pudding and smooth it with a spatula or knife.

2. Gently place the other, more attractive banana cake layer on top, banana-side up, and press down to even it out, pushing the buttercream out to almost the edges of the cake. Fill in the gaps with more buttercream so it is even with the edge of the layers, then smooth out the sides of cake with an offset spatula to form the crumb coat, leaving top of cake bare. Chill in refrigerator until the buttercream is firm, 30 minutes.

3. Use the remaining frosting to frost only the sides of the cake but not the top, leaving those gorgeous caramelized bananas exposed. If you feel like showing those bananas even more love, you can brush the top with a little simple syrup or melted apricot jam.

MOCHA CAKE WITH COFFEE FROSTING · {SERVES 12}

The moist, oil-based chocolate cake that stars in this layered confection is a standby both at the shop and under my cake dome at home. Thanks to a generous amount of cocoa and a healthy lashing of half-and-half, it develops a spongy texture that cradles the creamy chocolate pudding and delicate coffee buttercream frosting the way the nooks and crannies of an English muffin cradle a pat of butter. It all gets sealed together with a rich and creamy chocolate glaze.

FOR CHOCOLATE GLAZE:

2 teaspoons powdered gelatin

1 cup sugar

2/3 cup cocoa powder

1/4 cup heavy cream

FOR CAKE LAYERS:

2 cups sugar

1 3/4 cups all-purpose flour

1 cup cocoa powder

2 teaspoons baking soda

1 teaspoon baking powder

1 teaspoon salt

2 teaspoons instant espresso powder

1 cup canola oil

1 cup half-and-half

2 eggs

1 teaspoon vanilla extract

FOR COFFEE BUTTERCREAM FROSTING:

9 egg whites

1 cup plus 2 tablespoons sugar

4 sticks butter, softened

2 tablespoons instant espresso powder

FOR ASSEMBLY:

1 1/2 cups Chocolate Pudding (page 3)

CONTINUED

MAKE CHOCOLATE GLAZE:

1. Dissolve gelatin in 1 tablespoon cold water.

2. While gelatin is blooming, in a small saucepan whisk together ½ cup water, sugar, cocoa powder, and heavy cream.

3. Bring to a boil over medium-high heat, then reduce to medium and cook, whisking constantly, until mixture becomes a thin sauce, 4 minutes. Remove from heat.

4. Whisk bloomed gelatin into the hot mixture until dissolved. (Glaze will appear thin, but it will thicken up as it chills.)

5. Strain the mixture through a fine-mesh sieve into a bowl and chill in refrigerator until silky and pourable, 1–2 hours.

MAKE CAKE:

1. Preheat oven to 350°F. Coat two 8-inch round cake layer pans with cooking spray. Line the bottom of each pan with a round of parchment paper, spray the paper, and set aside.

2. In a large bowl whisk together sugar, flour, cocoa powder, baking soda, baking powder, and salt.

3. In a separate medium-sized bowl, dissolve instant espresso powder in 1 cup very hot water. Whisk in oil, half-and-half, eggs, and vanilla.

4. Add wet ingredients to dry ingredients and whisk until just incorporated.

5. Divide batter evenly between the two prepared pans and bake until the center springs back when pressed and inserted toothpick comes out clean, 35–40 minutes.

6. Let sit for 10 minutes, then invert onto a cooling rack and cool to room temperature, 1 hour. Using a serrated knife, gently slice domed top from cake layers to create evenly flat discs. Reserve domes for cake crumbs (see note page 112).

MAKE COFFEE BUTTERCREAM FROSTING:

1. Set the bowl of a stand mixer on top of a saucepan filled with simmering water and whisk egg whites and sugar until warm to the touch.

2. Return bowl with heated mixture to a stand mixer fitted with the whip attachment and whip at high speed until stiff and glossy, 4–5 minutes. (If buttercream separates, see Frosting 411 on page 98.)

3. Add butter 1 tablespoon at a time and whip until nice and fluffy, an additional 4–5 minutes.

4. Add espresso powder to buttercream and beat until completely dissolved, 1–2 minutes.

ASSEMBLE CAKE:

1. Place the first cake layer on a lazy Susan or large, flat plate. Transfer frosting to a pastry bag with a large, plain tip and pipe a ring of buttercream around the top of the cake about $1/4$ inch from the sides to create a wall, then fill the area inside the ring with the chocolate pudding and smooth out pudding with a spatula or knife.

2. Gently place the next cake layer on top and press down to even it out and push the buttercream out to almost the edges of the cake. Fill in the gaps with more buttercream so it is even with the edge of the layers, then smooth out with an offset spatula to create the crumb coat. Chill in refrigerator until buttercream solidifies, 30 minutes.

3. Center remaining buttercream on top of the cake. Using an offset spatula or a bench scraper, smooth the frosting outward into a thin layer, using frosting at edges of cake to frost sides completely.

4. Pour the glaze over the cake, starting around the sides and ending in the middle. Using a mini offset spatula or knife, quickly even out the glaze, covering any naked spots. Try not to touch the top after evening it out; you will mar the magic glossiness if you do (but it will taste awesome either way, so don't sweat it).

CONTINUED

5. Using a bench scraper or offset spatula on the sides of the cake only, rotate cake and, applying light pressure, pull and smooth glaze all around the cake to create a groovy, 1970s-style wood-grain effect.

Frosting 411

• • •

SOMETIMES, IN THE PROCESS OF WHIPPING FROSTING, THE MIXTURE CAN start to separate. Don't worry, my fair pastry mavens, it isn't you; it's the frosting. With a few simple repairs, you can rehab your buttercream, allowing it to come back together to form a beautiful frosting. If your buttercream looks like curdled milk instead of fluffing up as it is supposed to, place the mixer bowl back over a pot of simmering water to melt the butter mixture just a bit (you will see the buttercream begin to pull away from the sides of the bowl; don't melt it beyond this point). Return the bowl to the mixer fitted with the whip attachment and whip at high speed until light and fluffy. All will soon be right in the frosting universe!

LEMON LOVER'S CAKE · {SERVES 12}

I have a soft spot for the Crisco-frosted sheet cakes served at the birthday parties of my youth. My mom and I worked on this lemon-centric cake in part to pay homage to those cakes of yore. It has a bright triple lemon flavor thanks to the star ingredient's inclusion in every element, and that familiar texture thanks to the cake layers' spot-on crumb.

FOR THE CAKE:

½ cup whole milk

4 eggs

1 teaspoon vanilla extract

2¼ cups cake flour

1½ cups sugar

2 teaspoons baking powder

1 teaspoon salt

2 sticks butter, softened

1 tablespoon lemon juice

Finely grated zest of 1 lemon

FOR THE SYRUP:

½ cup sugar

½ cup lemon juice

FOR THE PUDDING FILLING:

½ teaspoon powdered gelatin

1½ cups Hevra's Lemon Obsession Pudding (page 11)

FOR THE LEMON BUTTERCREAM:

6 egg whites, room temperature

¾ cup plus 2 tablespoons sugar

4 sticks butter, softened, plus 4 tablespoons cold butter

4 tablespoons cream cheese

1½ cups Lemon Curd (page 12)

FOR GARNISH:

1 lemon, thinly sliced

CONTINUED

MAKE CAKE:

1. Preheat oven to 350°F. Grease two 8-inch cake layer pans and set aside.

2. In a medium bowl whisk the milk, eggs, and vanilla until combined and set aside.

3. In the bowl of a stand mixer fitted with the paddle attachment, combine the flour, sugar, baking powder, and salt and beat on low until just combined, 30 seconds. Increase speed to medium. Add butter a few tablespoons at a time and beat until the mixture looks pebbly, 1–2 minutes. Add lemon juice and lemon zest and beat an additional 30 seconds.

4. With the mixer on, add the milk mixture in a slow, steady stream. Raise speed to high and beat until light and fluffy, 3–4 minutes.

5. Pour into prepared pans and bake until layers spring back when touched, 20–22 minutes.

6. Remove from oven and let sit in pan for 10 minutes, then turn out onto a cooling rack set over a rimmed baking sheet and cool to room temperature, 30 minutes.

7. If necessary, using a serrated knife, gently slice domed top from cake layers to create two evenly flat discs. Reserve domes for cake crumbs (see note page 112)

8. Using a chopstick or a knife, poke holes in cake layers. Pour syrup over layers.

MAKE SYRUP:

While cake is baking or cooling, combine the sugar and lemon juice in a small saucepan, bring to a boil, reduce heat, and simmer until liquid is clear, 5 minutes. Remove from heat and set aside.

MAKE PUDDING FILLING:

1. In a small bowl dissolve gelatin in 1 tablespoon ice-cold water, 3–4 minutes.

2. In a medium microwave-safe bowl microwave 3 tablespoons pudding until hot, 30 seconds.

3. Whisk the dissolved gelatin into the hot pudding. Add to remaining pudding

and whisk quickly until fully incorporated (pudding will seem loose). Chill in refrigerator until pudding resolidifies, at least 1 hour.

MAKE BUTTERCREAM:

1. Set the bowl of a stand mixer atop a saucepan filled with simmering water and whisk egg whites and sugar until warm to the touch.

2. Return bowl with heated mixture to a stand mixer fitted with the whip attachment and whip at high speed until stiff and glossy, 4–5 minutes. (If buttercream seperates, see Frosting 411, page 98.)

3. Add the 4 sticks softened butter 1 tablespoon at a time, followed by the cream cheese 1 tablespoon at a time, and whip until nice and fluffy, an additional 4–5 minutes. Add the 4 tablespoons cold butter during the last 2 minutes to help the frosting come together.

4. Lower speed to medium and add the lemon curd ½ cup at a time, beating until just blended.

ASSEMBLE CAKE:

1. Place the first cake layer on a lazy Susan or large, flat plate. Transfer frosting to a pastry bag with a large, plain tip and pipe a ring of buttercream around the top of the cake about ¼ inch from the sides to create a wall. Fill the area inside the ring with the lemon pudding mixture and smooth out pudding with a spatula or knife.

2. Gently place the second cake layer on top and press down to even it out and push the buttercream out to almost the edges of the cake. Fill in the gaps with more buttercream so it is even with the edge of the layers, then smooth out with an offset spatula to create the crumb coat. Chill in refrigerator until buttercream solidifies, 30 minutes.

3. Center all but ½ cup of the remaining buttercream on top of the cake. Using an offset spatula or a bench scraper, smooth the frosting outward into a thin layer, using frosting at edges of cake to frost sides completely.

4. Use the remaining frosting to pipe 1-inch dots around the perimeter of the cake, leaving about 3 inches between dots.

5. Arrange lemon slices between dots.

VERY VANILLA CAKE · { SERVES 12 }

I'm so devoted to vanilla, I feel like an ambassador for the stuff. If you share my affections, you'll love this cake. It packs a quadruple vanilla whammy: vanilla syrup, springy vanilla cake, my signature Vanilla Pudding, and a vanilla buttercream frosting that has been known to make grown-ups cry and start composing poems. The recipe for the cake layers is adapted from Cook's Illustrated's The Best Recipe.

FOR VANILLA CAKE:

4 eggs

$\frac{1}{2}$ cup whole milk

$2\frac{1}{2}$ teaspoons vanilla extract

$2\frac{1}{4}$ cups cake flour

$1\frac{1}{2}$ cups sugar

2 teaspoons baking powder

1 teaspoon salt

2 sticks butter, softened

FOR VANILLA BUTTERCREAM FROSTING:

9 egg whites

1 cup plus 2 tablespoons sugar

4 sticks butter, softened

1 vanilla bean, split, seeds scraped out and reserved

2 teaspoons vanilla extract

FOR VANILLA SIMPLE SYRUP:

$\frac{1}{4}$ cup sugar

$\frac{1}{2}$ vanilla bean, split, seeds scraped out and reserved

FOR PUDDING LAYER:

2 cups Vanilla Pudding (page 4)

CONTINUED

MAKE CAKE:

1. Preheat oven to 350°F. Coat two 8-inch cake layer pans with cooking spray and line bottoms with rounds of parchment paper.

2. In a medium bowl whisk together the eggs, milk, and vanilla.

3. In the bowl of a stand mixer fitted with the paddle attachment, combine the flour, sugar, baking powder, and salt and mix on lowest speed until just incorporated. Add butter little by little and beat until the mixture looks pebbly, 1–2 minutes.

4. With the mixer running, add milk mixture and beat on medium speed until very fluffy, 2 minutes.

5. Divide batter among prepared pans and bake until a cake tester or wooden toothpick inserted into the center comes out clean, 25–30 minutes.

6. Remove from oven and let sit in pan for 10 minutes, then turn out onto a cooling rack and cool to room temperature, 30 minutes.

7. If necessary, using a serrated knife, gently slice domed top from cake layers to create evenly flat discs. Reserve domes for cake crumbs (see note page 112).

8. Using the same knife, carefully slice each layer horizontally into 2 layers of equal thickness, to yield 4 layers total; separate layers between sheets of wax paper.

MAKE FROSTING:

1. Set the bowl of a stand mixer on top of a saucepan filled with simmering water and whisk egg whites and sugar until warm to the touch, 2–3 minutes.

2. Return bowl with heated mixture to a stand mixer fitted with the whip attachment and whip at high speed until stiff and glossy, 4–5 minutes. (If buttercream separates, see Frosting 411, page 98.)

3. Add butter 1 tablespoon at a time and whip until nice and fluffy, an additional 5 minutes.

4. Add the vanilla bean, the scraped seeds, and the vanilla extract and beat 1 minute. Remove vanilla bean and discard.

1. While cake is baking or cooling, in a small saucepan bring ¼ cup water, sugar, and vanilla bean and seeds to a boil.

2. Remove from heat and cool to room temperature.

ASSEMBLE CAKE:

1. Place one of the cake layers on a lazy Susan or large, flat plate. Brush the top of the layer with some of the vanilla syrup. Transfer frosting to a pastry bag and pipe a ring of frosting around the top of the cake about ¼ inch from the sides to create a wall. Fill the area inside the ring with ⅔ cup of the pudding filling.

2. Place the next cake layer on top and gently press to even it out and push the frosting out almost to the edges of the cake. Brush cake layer with vanilla syrup, pipe another frosting ring, and fill with ⅔ cup of the pudding.

3. Repeat step 2 with the third cake layer, frosting ring, and additional ⅔ cup pudding.

4. Top with the fourth layer and brush the cake with vanilla syrup.

5. Fill in gaps between layers with additional frosting and smooth sides with a large offset spatula, creating the crumb coat. Chill in refrigerator until buttercream is solidified, about 30 minutes.

6. Center remaining buttercream on top of the cake. Using an offset spatula or a bench scraper, smooth the frosting outward into a thin layer, using frosting at edges of cake to frost sides completely. Alternatively, for a rustic effect, keep the sides unfrosted, as I like to do at the shop.

KEY LIME PUDDING
CHEESECAKE · { SERVES 12 }

Imagine the richest, craziest Key lime pie you've ever tasted, with its tongue-twisting tartness, and you'll get the idea behind this cheesecake. It's a huge hit at the shop; people seem to have Key lime radar, circling around the shop as soon as it comes out of the oven.

FOR GRAHAM CRACKER CRUST:

22 Graham Crackers (page 55) or 11 2 ½-by-5-inch sheets of store-bought graham crackers

5 tablespoons sugar (use 6 tablespoons if using store-bought crackers)

4 tablespoons butter, chilled, diced

FOR CHEESECAKE BASE:

4 ounces (½ cup) cream cheese, softened

3 tablespoons sugar

2 tablespoons whole milk

1 egg

2 tablespoons crème fraîche or sour cream

½ teaspoon vanilla extract

1½ teaspoons all-purpose flour

Finely grated zest of 3 Key limes or 1 regular lime

FOR PUDDING LAYER:

1 teaspoon powdered gelatin

1¼ cups Key Lime Pudding (page 39)

FOR ASSEMBLY:

Whipped Cream (optional, page 66)

MAKE CRUST:

1. Process graham crackers and sugar in a food processor until fine as dust, 1 minute.

CONTINUED

2. Add butter and process until fully incorporated, 30 seconds.

3. Liberally spray the bottom and sides of an 8-inch springform pan with cooking spray, then line the bottom with a piece of parchment paper.

4. Using your hands, press the mixture into the pan and 1½ inches up the sides until it forms a firm, even, solidly packed crust. Use your thumb to form sharp angles between the bottom and sides of the pan, which will make more space for your filling. Chill in refrigerator for 20 minutes.

MAKE CHEESECAKE BASE:

1. Preheat the oven to 325°F and place a rack in center of oven.

2. In a food processor pulse the cream cheese with the sugar until well blended, 1 minute. Add milk and egg and pulse until just combined, 5 pulses.

3. Add the crème fraîche, vanilla, flour, and lime zest and process until smooth, 30 seconds. Pour into prepared crust.

4. Bake until the cheesecake is just set, 22–25 minutes. Cool at room temperature for 10 minutes, then chill in refrigerator, uncovered, for 1 hour.

MAKE PUDDING LAYER:

1. In a small bowl dissolve powdered gelatin in 1 tablespoon cold water and set in refrigerator to bloom for 8 minutes.

2. In a medium microwave-safe bowl microwave 3 tablespoons pudding until hot, 30 seconds.

3. Whisk dissolved gelatin into heated pudding until smooth. Add remaining pudding and whisk quickly until fully incorporated.

ASSEMBLE CAKE:

Spread pudding layer on top of set cheesecake base and refrigerate for at least 1 hour. Dollop with whipped cream if desired.

BOSTON CREAM PIE · { SERVES 12 }

I love the way my job allows me to develop relationships with my customers, some of whom come in every day. This cake was a specific request from a couple of regulars, who asked me to re-create a dessert from their youth. Simple and traditional, it combines an old-fashioned vanilla cake with eggy custard and my killer chocolate glaze.

FOR VANILLA CAKE:

See recipe for Very Vanilla
  Cake layers, page 103

. . . .

FOR COCOA BUTTERCREAM FROSTING:

9 egg whites, room temperature

1 cup plus 2 tablespoons sugar

4 sticks butter, softened, plus
  4 tablespoons chilled butter

3/4 cup cocoa powder

1 vanilla bean, split, seeds scraped
  out and reserved

2 teaspoons vanilla extract

. . . .

FOR PUDDING FILLING:

1 teaspoon powdered gelatin

1 1/4 cups Boston Cream Pudding
  (page 30)

. . . .

FOR ASSEMBLY:

1 1/4 cups Chocolate Glaze (See Mocha
  Cake with Coffee Frosting, page 95)

MAKE CAKE:

Follow recipe for Very Vanilla Cake layers (page 103), but do not halve layers. (You should end up with 2 layers total.)

CONTINUED

MAKE FROSTING:

1. Set the bowl of a stand mixer atop a saucepan with simmering water and whisk egg whites and sugar until warm to the touch.

2. Return bowl with heated mixture to a stand mixer fitted with the whip attachment and whip at high speed until stiff and glossy, 4–5 minutes. (If buttercream separates, see Frosting 411, page 98.)

3. Add 4 sticks softened butter 1 tablespoon at a time and whip until nice and fluffy, an additional 4–5 minutes, adding the 4 tablespoons chilled butter during the last 2 minutes to help the frosting come together. Lower speed to medium, add the cocoa powder in 2 additions, return speed to high, and beat until fully incorporated, 30 seconds scraping down sides of bowl if necessary.

4. Add the vanilla bean, the scraped seeds, and the vanilla extract and beat 1 minute more. Remove vanilla bean and discard.

MAKE PUDDING FILLING:

1. In a small bowl dissolve gelatin in 1 tablespoon cold water and set in refrigerator to bloom for 8 minutes.

2. In a medium microwave-safe bowl microwave 3 tablespoons pudding until hot, 30 seconds.

3. Whisk dissolved gelatin into hot pudding. Add remaining pudding and whisk quickly until fully incorporated.

ASSEMBLE CAKE:

1. Place the first cake layer on a lazy Susan or large, flat plate. Transfer the frosting to a pastry bag with a large, plain tip and pipe a ring of buttercream around the top of the cake ¼ inch from the sides to create a wall. Fill the area inside the ring with the pudding and smooth out pudding with a spatula or knife.

CONTINUED

Boston Cream Pie

2. Gently place the next cake layer on top and press down to even it out and push the buttercream out to almost the edges of the cake. Fill in the gaps with more buttercream so it is even with the edge of the layers, then smooth out with an offset spatula to create the crumb coat. Chill in refrigerator until the buttercream is firm, 30 minutes.

3. Center the remaining buttercream on top of the cake. Using an offset spatula or a bench scraper, smooth the frosting outward into a thin layer, using frosting at edges of cake to frost sides completely.

4. Pour the glaze over the cake, starting around the sides and ending in the middle. Using a mini offset spatula or knife, quickly even out the glaze, covering any naked spots and forcing glaze to the sides. Try not to touch the top after evening it out; you will mar the magic glossiness if you do.

A Note About Cake Crumbs

"WASTE NOT, WANT NOT" IS A MOTTO EVERY CHEF LIVES BY, AND THE SAME is true at Puddin'. We try to repurpose every scrap—mostly because the scraps are so darn delicious. Take our cake layers. Leveling out the cakes has two major benefits. One: flattening the cakes makes the frosting process easier. Two: leftovers! The domed tops become the cake crumbs used in our parfaits. Doing this will save you time and get you one step closer to dessert heaven with less work. Best of all, the crumbles can be sealed in an airtight bag and stored in the freezer for 2–3 months.

COCONUT CREAM CUSTARD TART • { SERVES 12 }

This beautiful, exotic tart was developed by my very talented mother, Hevra. It's the only cake that calls for its own pudding instead of one of my standard recipes, but it's so good that I had to include it. This tart is best eaten within a couple hours of assembling, otherwise you run the risk of sogginess.

FOR THE COCONUT CUSTARD:

3/4 cup sugar

4 egg yolks

One 13 1/2-ounce can coconut milk

1/2 cup whole milk

1/4 cup cornstarch

1/4 cup crème fraîche

FOR THE CRUST:

1 stick butter, chilled and cut into 8 pieces

3 tablespoons confectioners' sugar

1 1/4 cups all-purpose flour

1/4 cup unsweetened dried coconut, lightly toasted

Pinch of salt

1 egg yolk

1 tablespoon coconut milk or heavy cream

FOR THE BAKED CUSTARD:

1/2 cup sugar

2 tablespoons butter, softened

1 tablespoon all-purpose flour

1 egg, lightly beaten

1/4 cup buttermilk

1 1/2 tablespoons coconut milk

1/4 cup unsweetened dried coconut

1/4 teaspoon vanilla extract

FOR THE MERINGUE:

1 1/2 teaspoons cornstarch

1/2 cup sugar

1/4 teaspoon cream of tartar

5 egg whites, at room temperature

1/2 teaspoon vanilla extract

Pinch of salt

CONTINUED

MAKE THE COCONUT CUSTARD:

1. In a medium bowl whisk the sugar and egg yolks until thick and pale, 1 minute.

2. In a medium saucepan vigorously whisk the coconut milk, milk, and cornstarch until the cornstarch is dissolved.

3. Heat over medium heat, whisking constantly, until very warm but not boiling, 3–4 minutes.

4. Very slowly add the hot milk mixture into the yolk-sugar mixture, whisking constantly so as not to curdle the eggs.

5. Pour the milk-egg mixture back into the pot, return to the heat, and cook, whisking constantly, until mixture is just boiling and is thick and creamy, 6–7 minutes.

6. Strain through a fine-mesh strainer into a medium bowl, cover surface with plastic wrap, and chill completely, either in the refrigerator or in an ice bath.

7. Whisk the crème fraîche into the chilled pudding.

MAKE THE CRUST:

1. In the bowl of a stand mixer fitted with the paddle attachment, beat the butter and confectioners' sugar at low speed until just combined, 20 seconds.

2. In a medium bowl toss together the flour, coconut, and salt. Add to the bowl of the stand mixer and beat until just combined, 30 seconds, scraping down sides of mixer if necessary. Add the yolk and the coconut milk and beat until just combined.

3. Gather the dough into a flat disk 5 inches in diameter (dough will be sticky, with pea-sized pieces of butter visible). Wrap in plastic wrap and chill in refrigerator at least 1 hour.

CONTINUED

Coconut Cream Custard Tart

4. On a lightly floured surface, roll the dough into a 12-inch circle and transfer to a greased 8- or 9-inch tart pan with a removable bottom.

5. Trim the dough to fit the edges of the pan, and chill the dough in refrigerator for at least an hour and up to 24 hours.

MAKE THE BAKED CUSTARD:

1. Preheat the oven to 350°F. In the bowl of a stand mixer fitted with the whisk attachment, cream the sugar and butter on medium-high speed until light and fluffy, 4 minutes. Turn off the mixer and add the flour and egg. Beat until just incorporated, then add the buttermilk, coconut milk, coconut, and vanilla and beat until smooth, 1 minute.

2. Remove the chilled tart pan from the refrigerator. Using a pastry docker or fork, poke holes on the bottom of the crust.

3. Cover the crust with parchment and fill the crust with pie weights or dried beans.

4. Bake until just set, 15–20 minutes, and remove pie weights and parchment. Pour the custard mixture into the hot crust and bake until custard is set and lightly puffy, 20–25 minutes.

5. Spread the chilled coconut custard on top of the baked custard, smoothing with an offset spatula.

MAKE THE MERINGUE:

1. Preheat oven to 350°F. In a small saucepan dissolve the cornstarch in ¼ cup cold water. Heat mixture over medium-high heat, stirring constantly, until the mixture has boiled and thickened, 2–3 minutes. Set aside to cool at room temperature.

2. In a small bowl, combine the sugar and cream of tartar.

3. In the bowl of a stand mixer fitted with the whisk attachment, beat the egg whites on medium speed until frothy, 30 seconds. Increase speed to medium-high, add the sugar mixture 1 tablespoon at a time, and beat until the mixture forms soft peaks, 2–3 minutes. With mixer still running, add the vanilla and salt. Add the cooled cornstarch mixture 1 tablespoon at a time and beat until the meringue forms medium peaks and is glossy, 3–4 minutes.

4. Top the filled tart with the meringue, using the back of a spoon to create decorative peaks.

5. Bake until meringue is browned, 10 minutes. Cool on a wire rack for 30 minutes. Serve at room temperature or chill in refrigerator up to 2 hours.

HAZELNUT CREPE CAKE

{ MAKES 20-21 CREPES }

Hats off to my mom, Hevra, who created this fanciful crepe cake for the store. Soaked hazelnuts left over from my Nutella Pudding (page 23) are used in the crepe batter. Once cooked, the lacy crepes cradle the rich pudding, punctuated every once in a while with a touch of raspberry jam. When making this cake, be sure not to overfill the layers with pudding, and make the pudding as level as possible to avoid a lopsided cake.

FOR CREPES:

2 cups whole milk

4 eggs

2 cups flour

2 tablespoons granulated sugar

1 cup soaked hazelnuts
   (see Nutella Pudding, page 23)

2 teaspoons cinnamon

Generous pinch freshly
   grated nutmeg

Generous pinch ground cloves

1/8 teaspoon salt

4 tablespoons butter, melted

FOR ASSEMBLY:

3 tablespoons seedless raspberry jam,
   melted

1 cup Nutella Pudding (page 23)

1/3 cup raw sugar

MAKE CREPES:

1. In a blender combine the milk, eggs, 1/2 cup water, flour, sugar, hazelnuts, cinnamon, nutmeg, cloves, and salt and blend on high until smooth, 30 seconds (blend in 2 batches if necessary).

2. Transfer the batter to a bowl, cover, and refrigerate for at least 1 hour and up to overnight. (The batter should have the consistency of heavy cream.)

3. Strain the batter through a fine mesh strainer, discarding any solids.

4. Heat a nonstick 9-inch skillet or crepe pan over medium heat and lightly brush the skillet with some of the melted butter. Using a small ladle or measuring cup, pour ¼ cup batter into the heated pan, swirl to coat, and pour off any remaining batter. Cook until the top is no longer wet and the underside is lightly browned, 30 seconds to 1 minute.

5. Flip the crepe and cook until the underside is cooked, just a few more seconds. Place crepe on a plate and continue with remaining batter, brushing crepe pan with additional melted butter as necessary and stacking the crepes between layers of plastic wrap once slightly cooled.

ASSEMBLE CAKE:

1. Arrange a crepe on a plate and lightly brush the crepe with 1 tablespoon of the warm raspberry jam. Top with another crepe.

3. With a small offset spatula or butter knife, spread a scant tablespoon of pudding evenly over the crepe, pressing down to even out filling between crepes. Continue with the crepe-and-pudding layering procedure (*without* jam) until the ninth layer. On the ninth crepe, spread 1 additional tablespoon melted jam and top with another crepe. Repeat the crepe-and-pudding layering procedure (*without* jam) until the second-to-last (17th) layer.

4. Top the final jam-filled layer with the last crepe. Cover loosely with plastic wrap and chill in refrigerator 1 hour.

5. Transfer to a serving plate. Sprinkle the top with the sugar. Using a brûlée torch, lightly brown until caramelized. (Alternatively, place the sugared cake under the broiler, for 30 seconds.)

PUDDING POPS

COME SUMMERTIME, PEOPLE FLOCK TO THE SHOP CRAVING SOMETHING to help tame the beast that is the New York summer. And while it's true that a cup of plain old pudding usually does the trick, it's our pudding pops that define the season. Nothing eases the swelter like a velvety bite of frozen pudding on a stick, in one of our original flavor combinations. Using pudding you've already made, you can assemble these pops in advance, ready to enjoy at a moment's notice.

Pop Preparation

- Pudding pops require a good, long rest in the freezer before fully solidifying. Don't even think of eating one of your creations less than 6 hours after freezing; ideally, wait a full 24 hours before unmolding and serving.

- All flavor combinations here are merely suggestions. If you feel eggnog pudding would be better than vanilla, or banana instead of pineapple, who am I to stop you?

- In the shop, our pudding pops are made in silicone molds that create classic ridged, rectangular pops. If you can't find them, any 4-ounce popsicle mold will do.

- To turn any of our pops into chocolate-dipped confections, see recipe for Chocolate Lacquer (page 125) and instructions on How to Lacquer a Pudding Pop (page 124).

- When unmolding, if pops refuse to release from their molds, simply dip molds into a bowl of warm water for 5 seconds, then try releasing the pops. Return to the warm water for another 5 seconds and then loosen with a knife if necessary.

BANANA SPLIT POPS • MAKES 6 POPS

A frozen sundae on a stick, this pop is the smartphone of desserts: it's compact and you'll want to have one on you at all times!

½ cup Vanilla Pudding (page 4)

¼ cup Dulce de Leche Pudding (page 27)

¾ cup Chocolate Pudding (page 3)

1½ cups Banana Pudding (page 8)

1. In a small bowl whisk together the vanilla pudding and dulce de leche pudding until smooth.

2. In each mold, layer in order half of the chocolate pudding, half of the banana pudding, and half of the vanilla–dulce de leche pudding mixture. Repeat. Center a wooden popsicle stick in each pop

3. Freeze mold completely, at least 6 hours.

. . . .

COOKIES AND CREAM POPS • MAKES 6 POPS

The saltiness of the cookie crumbles mixed with vanilla pudding creates an alluring yin-yang that makes this pop a favorite with my customers.

1 ¾ cups Vanilla Pudding (page 4)

4 Chocowich Bits cookies (page 50), crumbled

In a medium bowl gently fold pudding and cookies together. Spoon into molds. Center a wooden popsicle stick in each pop. Freeze completely, at least 6 hours.

How to Lacquer a Pudding Pop

REFREEZE: Once you've released your pops from their molds, return the pops to the freezer on a parchment-lined plate or baking sheet for 10 minutes to refreeze any slightly melted portions.

PICK YOUR VESSEL: Since the goal is to enrobe the entire pop in one fell swoop, a taller, narrower vessel—such as a coffee mug or even a simple drinking glass—is an ideal dipping receptacle. Just make sure the vessel is about 1 inch wider than the pop on each side to guarantee easy, uncrowded dipping.

GET DIPPING: Make sure your lacquer is truly at room temperature; if your kitchen's really hot or really cold, do something about it! Pour the lacquer into the vessel. Then, working one at a time, dip each pop into the lacquer and lift out, and dangle the pop at an angle, letting any excess lacquer drizzle back into the dipping vessel. Lacquer will begin to harden almost immediately.

FREEZE AGAIN: For best results, after dipping return pops to the parchment-lined plate or baking sheet for at least 10 minutes to allow lacquer to harden. Eat and enjoy, or wrap individually in wax or parchment paper and store in freezer for up to 1 month.

CHOCOLATE LACQUER · MAKES 2 CUPS

Inspired by Magic Shell, the squeezable liquid that morphs from fluid to solid within seconds of hitting a scoop of ice cream, this easy-to-make topping turns any of our Pudding Pops into luscious chocolate-dipped treats in a flash. Make sure to use a neutral-flavored oil, such as canola or safflower.

2 cups chopped dark chocolate

1 cup vegetable oil

In a double boiler combine the chocolate and oil and heat until melted and smooth, 2–3 minutes. Remove from heat and let cool to room temperature before dipping pops, at least one hour. Extra lacquer can be stored in fridge in a microwave-safe container. Before serving heat in microwave until re-liquefied; then cool to room temperature before dipping. Lacquer will keep up to one month if stored in an airtight container in the refrigerator.

LEMON-RASPBERRY POPS · MAKES 6 POPS

⅓ cup fresh raspberries

1 tablespoon sugar

½ teaspoon vanilla extract

3 cups Hevra's Lemon Obsession Pudding (page 11)

In a medium bowl gently fold together the raspberries, sugar, and vanilla. Macerate for 30 minutes. Add lemon pudding and fold gently to combine. Spoon into molds and center a wooden Popsicle stick in each pop. Freeze completely, at least 6 hours.

MINT CHIP POPS • MAKES 6 POPS

By far my favorite pop, this one transports me straight back to childhood with just one bite. I've been a mint-chipper practically since birth, and this is the dessert you'd find in my frozen time capsule.

3 cups Desperate Measures Mint Chip Pudding (page 33)

Spoon pudding into molds and center a wooden Popsicle stick in each pop. Freeze completely, at least 6 hours.

. . . .

PEANUT BUTTER FUDGE POPS • MAKES 6 POPS

I'll tell you what I tell all my customers: this pop is epic, and that's all you need to know.

2¼ cups Peanut Butter Pudding (page 25)

⅓ cup Fudge Sauce (page 61)

2 cups Chocolate Lacquer (page 125)

½ cup roasted salted peanuts

1. In a medium bowl gently fold together the pudding and fudge sauce.

2. Spoon into molds and center a wooden Popsicle stick in each pop. Freeze, at least 6 hours.

3. Dip each pop into chocolate lacquer. Let the excess drip away, garnish with roasted peanuts, and freeze the chocolate-enrobed pops on single layers of wax paper until solid. Wrap in wax or parchment paper to store in freezer.

PIÑA COLADA POPS   •   MAKES 6 POPS

Coconut pops can sometimes get icy, but a shot of rum helps balance the mix, resulting in pops that freeze up smooth and creamy.

2½ cups Pineapple Pudding (page 37)

½ cup coconut milk

1½ teaspoons white or coconut rum

½ teaspoon vanilla extract

10 Vanilla Wafers (page 57), crushed

1. In a medium bowl whisk together pudding, coconut milk, rum, and vanilla.

2. Remove ½ cup of this mixture and combine with the crushed wafers in a separate bowl; let stand 5 minutes to moisten.

3. Fold moistened cookie mush back into the reserved pudding mixture. Spoon into molds and center a wooden Popsicle stick in each pop. Freeze, at least 6 hours.

THE RUGGED MAN POPS   •   MAKES 6 POPS

From disaster comes innovation. Right after St. Patrick's Day, a batch of Butterscotch Pudding didn't turn out so bueno—the taste was fabulous but the texture was too loose. In a fit of desperation I threw some leftover chocolate cake crumbs in with the pudding, added some Irish cream liqueur, and voilà! A deliciously addictive pop was born.

2¼ cups Butterscotch Pudding (page 5)

¾ cup chocolate cake crumbs (see note page 112)

3 tablespoons Irish cream liqueur

In a medium bowl gently fold together all ingredients. Spoon into molds and center a wooden Popsicle stick in each pop. Freeze completely, at least 6 hours.

ACKNOWLEDGMENTS

Mom, thanks for teaching me everything I know, for knowing everything, for being my partner in crime, my main recipe tester, my history book, and my human cookbook. This book wouldn't be anything without your help and collaboration. You're more talented than any celebrity chef out there, and I'm not just saying that because you're my mom.

Dad, Thanks for being my rock, for helping me stay inspired and on the straight and narrow, for forgiving me when I used up all of your scotch and made a mess in the sink, for being my "poison taster," for teaching me what it means to be a good businessperson and a good person in general, for your enthusiasm, for all your amazing advice and lectures (yes, I do listen!), and, most of all, for being my dad.

Emmett. Thanks for seeing me as me, for cooking me dinner after a long day at work, for being my drawing buddy, my movie buddy (even if it's only ever at home), and my sibling.

Hana Landes. Thanks for giving me the opportunity to create this book, for believing in the project as much as I do. Who knew when you came into the shop on our first day in business where we would be today? I hope that the finished product is everything you wanted it to be and more. I can't wait to do more projects with you!

Adeena Sussman. Thanks for being my friend and food buddy. This book wouldn't have been nearly as much fun had I written it with someone else. You're a wonderful person, and one of a kind indeed. I loved collaborating with you, and you really know how to light up a room!

Noah. I don't think either of us realized this could be this big on that fateful day when creative sparks first flew. You have the patience of a saint for sticking around through the rough times. It will be so much fun to grow this shop with you; I can't wait to see where it takes us!

Nick. Although we don't see each other that often, it makes me happy to know you are keeping tabs on everything. I always love your emails filled with encouraging quotes. They may only be a couple of sentences long, but they have the impact of a thousand paragraphs.

Doug. Thanks for guiding the shop in the direction it needed to go, and for your business expertise, for checking in on us, for helping us keep an eye on details, and for forgiving me when I spelled your name wrong every single time the first couple of months.

Larissa Drekonja. Thanks for understanding my way of thinking. You're tough on the outside, and extremely wise and thoughtful on the inside. You never cease to amaze me with your ideas and creativity.

Team Spiegel & Grau. Thanks so much for all the hard work and love you put into the making of this book. Barbara Bachman, you truly captured the style of Puddin' with so much class. Greg Mollica, the cover is absolutely tantalizing; I could lick it. And Julie and Cindy, thank you for giving me the opportunity to create and work on this project. It was truly an honor and a privilege to work with all of you.

Marc Gerald. Thank you for your belief in the shop and in the book.

Ben Fink. Thank you for the beautiful photos you took for the book. You are a shining star, and I loved watching you work your magic with the camera, hearing about all the places you've traveled to, and seeing your many projects come to life.

Brenden Guastella. Thanks for helping me start off on the right foot and for being honest and straightforward every single time. You are a great teacher and a kind soul. I'm so glad we met and that you are along for this adventure with us.

Mercedes De Rosas. Your vision and skill translated my ideas into a beautiful shop. After all that tedious construction, we emerged as friends, and I am so grateful for that. You are a strong woman whom I greatly admire and look up to as a role model.

Tim Zydek. Somewhere in that boyish grin lives an old man with a wicked potty mouth and a wise head. Without you the shop wouldn't be nearly as organized as it is now. You know how to calm me down, even if that means scaring the #&$* out of me by popping out of nowhere. You are a great guy, friend, and teammate . . . even if you look like Ryan Gosling.

Team Puddin'. To everyone with Puddin' now, or who was part of our team in the past, thank you. We are a unit, and I love all of you with all my heart! You brighten up the shop with your charm and charisma—and specials. You are my family. I did such a good job.

John Nihoff. Thanks for being my mentor at the CIA and for seeing in me what most people didn't. Just you wait and see—the next time you judge *Iron Chef*, I hope it's me you're watching. I'm going to rock that kitchen!

Melenie Mueller and Ashley Martin. Thanks for being some of the best gal pals I've ever had, and for accepting and loving me for who I am before the shop and even after, and for looking out for me and keeping me grounded. I look forward to taking you guys on the best shopping spree and to having some of the most fabulous tea parties ever.

—*The ever-loving Clip*

INDEX

Page references in *italics* refer to illustrations.